Tarot for Grownups

Tarot for Grownups

Amythyst Raine

DODONA
BOOKS

Winchester, UK
Washington, USA

First published by Dodona Books, 2013
Dodona Books is an imprint of John Hunt Publishing Ltd., Laurel House, Station Approach,
Alresford, Hants, SO24 9JH, UK
office1@jhpbooks.net
www.johnhuntpublishing.com
www.dodona-books.com

For distributor details and how to order please visit the 'Ordering' section on our website.

Text copyright: Amythyst Raine 2012

ISBN: 978 1 78099 599 1

A CIP catalogue record for this book is available from the British Library.

Design: Stuart Davies

Printed and bound by CPI Group (UK) Ltd, Croydon, CR0 4YY

We operate a distinctive and ethical publishing philosophy in all
areas of our business, from our global network of authors to
production and worldwide distribution.

CONTENTS

This book is dedicated to my kids,
all seven, for their patience, encouragement,
and enthusiasm.

Preface

The first deck of tarot cards I had gave me fits. Quite frankly, I became so frustrated during my first few attempts at reading tarot that I almost gave up on the whole idea, packed the cards away and said, "Thanks, but no thanks." It was a painful process of peering intently at the unfamiliar card before me and then scanning this tiny white booklet with print the same size as the directions on an aspirin bottle. I sat in rapt concentration trying to figure out how this pat neutral explanation even came close to fitting me and my situation.

I could've quit, given up on the whole idea of reading the cards, packed that first deck away and never given it another thought. But it didn't work that way. I was drawn back to that deck of cards again and again, and then to other decks, other images, other tarot artists. As my collection of tarot decks grew, along with the images and artistry, my understanding and ability to read the cards grew as well.

For one thing, I stopped pigeonholing the meanings of the cards. I stopped labeling a card simply based on a traditional book meaning.

For instance, the three of cups, whether it appeared in the Hanson/Roberts Deck, or the Goddess Tarot, or even The Medieval Scapini Tarot, the general meaning was the same: a celebration, merriment, jubilation. I discovered, through a slow dawning realization which came from doing frequent readings, that no, the three of cups does *not* always mean a celebration, merriment, or even jubilation. Sometimes it has told me of scattered hyper frenetic energy that was destructive and volatile. Once the three of cups whispered in my ear of deceit and trickery, telling me to warn the querent about people who came to her in the guise of 'friend'. And occasionally it has spoken of good fortune, or the unexpected, coming in 'three's'.

Each card may give you a different message for every reading. In this way, the tarot is as fluid and changeable as the waves of the ocean, or wisps of clouds in the sky. You can never look at a single card the same way twice, for in the brief span of seconds you look away— it changes.[11]

In my first book, *"Tarot: A Witch's Journey"*, I take an in-depth non-traditional look at each card. For more information go to: http://wytchymystique.wordpress.com/my-books

Life's Cubbyholes

Love/Relationships/Family

I'm amazed at just how many cards in a tarot deck can have significance where love, relationships, and family are concerned. This seems to be the dominating subject for most of the readings I do. And this makes sense. If we're not successfully connected to those we love, life isn't being lived the way it was meant to be.

Some of the following cards are 'traditional' to these topics, and some aren't, and that's just the way the ball rolls.

Two/wands: This is the old married couple. There's no hot sex, and often no sex at all. This card whispers about co-dependent relationships, one of the partners usually enabling the other in whatever sort of issues are involved. It can also tell you when one partner is having an affair and the other may be pretending not to notice, the old 'head in the sand' deal "If I don't acknowledge this affair, I won't have to face all those ugly issues in my marriage." Eventually, the character on this card is going to have to turn his ass around and look at what's happening. The cowardly act of denial only puts off confrontations and obvious decisions, it doesn't make them go away.

Two/cups: There's no hot sex here either, but the relationship is stable and normal. There's that word again, normal, meaning as in how society would view it. He works nine to five, or an evening shift at the plant. She might work, or if she doesn't, she has her ladies clubs and charities, her little social circle. He might bowl on Friday nights, or play golf on Sunday. Is this little suburban dream real, or are these characters caught in some nightmarish Stepford scenario? For that answer, you'll want to watch the cards that are coming up around the Two of Cups. If this is just a matter of role playing, a cover-up for darker personalities and secret desires, the cards will give you the real picture. They'll squeal like a mob snitch under torture.

Seven/cups: When it comes to relationships, there will be lots of decisions to be made, often life-changing, in-your-face, nothing will ever be the same decisions. As smart as the most intelligent person is, when it comes to decisions about relationships, they can be retarded beyond belief. No matter how exuberant, deer-caught-in-the-headlights, over-the-moon happy someone might be about a new union, an engagement, a promise for the future; if cards are coming up telling you there is a shit-load of crap on the horizon, you'd better say something. Temper it if you have to, but don't bury the obvious and then close your eyes to wait for the explosion; because a few days, weeks, months later, this person is going to come back to you all pinched and pale, teary-eyed and disillusioned, and they will say, "Why didn't you tell me."

Three/swords: Someone is having an affair. If it happens to be the querent him/herself, don't expect them to admit it. If you even breathe this word..."affair"...they will look at you with unabashed wide-open innocent eyes and act all shocked and virginal. The alternative is that their partner is cheating on them. Don't go there. But know that someone in this relationship is having an affair, unless The Lovers comes up with this card, and then it's not an affair, it's a ménage-a-trois. Don't go there either.

Ten/cups: Think "Ozzy & Harriet", "Leave it to Beaver", "The Donna Reed Show". It's almost too good to be true, or at least so idealistic that it could make you puke. If it really is good, then hey, more power to them, way to go. But if it isn't, what are they trying to hide? I'm a realist, and I've very seldom met 'the perfect family', or better yet, 'the perfectly happy family'. I'm also a cynic, so I'm not sure I believe there is such a thing as a family that is not dysfunctional in some way. But you know what? Sometimes it works. No matter how twisted the set-up might look to the rest of the world, for this group of people, it actually works. If that's the case, leave it alone.

Five/cups: Incredibly deep, penetrating, all encompassing sadness. In relationships there are incredible highs, a euphoria that you may not have ever experienced before. But just as the highs are super high; if it all goes to hell in a hand basket, the lows will be beyond anything you could imagine. I have met an alarming number of people who are wasting large chunks of their lives mourning about relationships that just didn't work out, blotting out all of life going on around them to dwell on 'what if's', blind to all the possibilities and simple joys surrounding them, consumed by their obsession. Perhaps this is the real sadness.

Four/wands: A party is afoot when this card comes up; either a wedding for a couple, or something big for an entire family, some sort of milestone. This card breathes a sigh of relief. It says that even though the going may not always be smooth, life will have it's special moments, when we can stand still, hold hands, and connect. Simple as that.

Ace/cups: I've noticed that this card almost always comes up for someone who is alone, romantically speaking, and that's because this card heralds a new relationship on the horizon. Love is coming, just hold on to your hat, listen for that special voice, watch for those eyes that captivate you. You'll know it when you see it, when you hear it, when you feel it. That's what the Ace of Cups says, be ready, open, willing to take it all in and embrace the moment.

There are many types of relationships, and many types of people who come and go from our lives in a variety of ways and at various stages.

I was doing readings in a book store once, when a young girl, about twelve years old, came into my booth. I generally don't read for children, but this was a Harry Potter in-store book party, so parents were at hand.

She sat down across from me, very wide-eyed, quiet, and expectant, absolutely adorable. As I turned the cards for her, this card, the Ace of Cups, came up (reversed). I was hesitant at first, then I told her, *"This card, when it comes up this way, often means that someone we love has left. But it's not necessarily a bad thing, it just means that they've 'gone away' for a while."*

Her eyes opened wide in amazement, and the expression on her face was like a light bulb going on. She opened her little mouth and enthusiastically began telling me about her cousin, her dearest friend, how they'd been together ever since they were 'little'; and how her cousin and her cousin's family had just moved away. She told me how sad she was, how much she missed her cousin and all about plans to visit each other. She prattled on and on, and I just sat and let her talk.

When she left my booth, she met her mother on the other side with a high-pitched incredulous voice, *"She said that someone I loved had **left**, but that it was okay!"* I could hear her enthusiastically talking to her mother, her chattering little voice fading as they walked away.

Six/swords: Traditionally this is the *'divorce card'*, but there isn't really anything traditional about it. Someone wants out of a marriage or commitment, or someone may have begun the legal technicalities already, even before the boat pictured on this card left port. The six of swords almost spits disdain, the characters on the card mirroring the reality of a situation with an almost nonchalant 'it was bound to happen' air. Optimists might howl for attempts at reconciliation, counseling, or therapy of some kind. But really, and realistically, don't bother. If the mutiny is run by a wife, she's sick of the sight of 'him', is repulsed by his touch, can't stand the sound of his voice, and dreads the tick-tock of the clock that will bring him home at the end of the day. Suggesting to this woman that she seek marriage counseling and try and save her marriage would be akin to asking her to eat her own vomit. Let it go. No use beating a dead horse. If the mutiny comes from a husband, he's most likely already got his sights set on something pink and luscious in his future, and if not, he's the poor bastard I spoke of above.

Two/swords: This card lets us know when two people are not getting along. The head-butting can get as vicious and deadly as a couple of old stags fighting it out in the woods, and the whole situation will smell just as randy. It also doesn't help when one of the parties is in complete denial and tries to play along as though the rarer and rarer moments of normalcy are the focus of their world. Eventually, when those moments of normalcy disappear altogether, and they will, what's left? Empty rooms, hollow hallways, and great spaces filled with loneliness. It's too late then, to pull your head from your ass.

The Lovers: This is the *"hot sex, I can't keep my hands off you, fuck me again card"*. It usually pops up when a new relationship is on the horizon, or someone is already immersed in the frenzied early stages of a relationship. They can't get enough of each other, not enough kissing, not enough talking, not enough touching, not enough sex. When they're not together, they're thinking about being together. Every hour they are away from each other feels like an eternity, and when they are together hours seem to pass like minutes. The thing is, and no one caught up in this incredible connection will believe you, but the thing is, this won't last. It can't. It would be physically impossible to maintain this height of passion, this intensity of feeling, this myopic obsessive compulsion for another human being.-

But it is incredible, absolutely undeniably incredible, so enjoy it while it lasts.

Ten/pentacles: Oh, gawds, there's money floating around, usually lots of money, and everyone expects to dip their hand in the pot and come out with a fistful of afternoon margaritas and leisure time. My experience has been that lots of money generally leads to lots of greed. Forget family loyalty.-

I've been unfortunate enough to experience the ten of pentacles up-close and personal; and although it was unpleasant, it was also fascinating to see how the psychology of the individuals involved played into each other, where the chips fell, who aligned with whom. Who has a backbone and the individuality that goes along with it? Who are the sniveling cowards who have calluses on their knees from spending too much time kissing someone's ass? Which characters will do what's right, and which characters will do what they're told? When this card shows up, it will be like a bag of dog shit blowing up in your face.

The thing is, if you look very closely at this card, *very closely*, it will actually reveal some of the players. You'll be able to identify them, and you may even pick up on their motives, their reasons for blatant hatred, back-stabbing, and plotting. It's a dog eat dog world in the matter of the almighty dollar. May the best man win, or at least survive the skirmish.

Eight/cups: Someone wants out, someone is leaving, someone has left, someone is running away, someone is in denial, someone is giving up, someone wants to forget the whole thing.

Elvis has left the building.

The one thing I find most disturbing when this card comes up is the usually hopeful set of eyes peering at me from across the table and from over the cards. It's almost always a woman, and she's almost always madly in love and enamored with some guy who couldn't give a rat's ass about her or a relationship. I can't very well say, "Forget it honey, this guy is moving on to new pastures." But that's exactly what's happening.

Well, I read for a man once who had two women and wanted to keep them both. He couldn't decide which one he wanted to stay with and which one he wanted to leave. Quite frankly, this card could've reached up and smacked him in the face, and he still would've been oblivious to the truth and the inevitable ending. This type of character never sees the bus coming, till he finds it's tread marks all over his ego.

Three/cups: This is the 'party hardy' card. Someone is having a good ole' time, the spirits are flowing, and I'm talking liquid spirits here, and there is something to celebrate. If not, any excuse will do.

This card strikes me in a variety of ways, and yes, these are generalities, but generalities tend to be the norm, so bear with me.

When it comes up for a young adult: Whoa, if their parents knew what they were up to, they'd be in a blind panic. This is when the 'party hardy' aspect usually comes into play, big time. If it's a girl sitting across from me, I hope she's on a good birth control. If it's a boy, I hope to god he won't drink and drive.

I feel all tired and played out just looking at this card. I don't like to look at anything traditionally, including the three of cups.

So, say there might be some sort of family celebration coming up. Strangely enough, when this has actually been the case, more often than not, instead of the enthusiasm that you would expect to see from a client, you find instead a sense of dread, or at least enthusiasm that seems feigned.

Family gatherings are kind of like a trial by fire. I have never, *never*, met a family who was not dysfunctional in some unique way. The only so-called 'normal' families that you are going to find will be on "Leave it to Beaver" or "Father Knows Best", and

Robert Young would've driven me nuts with his eternal smile and over-the-top optimism. I would never have satisfied him as the obedient little housewife with starched apron, a string of pearls, and those prim little house dresses. Underneath it all, I'd go commando.

The celebrations heralded by the three of cups are milestones, and the one thing that unnerves everyone about milestones is the passage of time, change, and the illumination of human mortality. Nothing lasts forever, including us.

Six/cups: Mists of time, faces from our past, ancestry, heritage, memories...

A little farmhouse in South Dakota, and Grandma Smith's kitchen.

Smells: The scent of roasters of home-fried chicken and gravy, the pungent smell of creamed cucumbers laced with onions, coffee perking in an aluminum coffeepot, Grandpa's pipe, Aunt Alpha's perfume, corncobs burning in Grandma's old-fashioned cook stove.

Sounds: The hum of voices in conversation, some soft, some loud, all laced with laughter and shouted questions. Plates and silverware clinking. Aunt Alpha's unmistakable distinctive laugh rising above everything else. And Grandma's voice, always punctuating the conversation, asking if anyone needs anything.

Sights: Ancient Aunt Lizzie sitting all by herself in the corner, silently hand-pitting blue-berries for a pie, a look of intense concentration on her beautiful deeply lined face. Her white bun squashed into a hairnet, dark collar-laced dress, little old lady black-laced shoes, opaque stockings, and purple stained fingertips.

This is the six of cups.

Employment

The most precious and irreplaceable commodity that we have is our time, and a great huge whopping chunk of this time is going to be spent at work. Most people I've seen have a job and hate it, or they don't have a job and want one. Either way, if employment is an issue in your life, it will dominate the landscape.

Three/pentacles: Get the led out; put the pedal to the medal; hit the grindstone...work, work, work. That's the essence of this card, and it's this topic that is dominated by its energy. Once in a while it can be a reflection of how you interact with fellow employees, but it's generally a peaceful and mellow interaction, where the cogs are running smoothly and steady progression is being made.

This card wreaks of routine, repetition, timeliness...and sometimes boredom.

Three/wands: There's a deal in the works, probably involving more than two parties, and it's usually something that's been in the works for some time. The thing is, who's doing what with whom, business wise of course. There's always one player who seems to have their hand under the table in someone's lap, stroking the kitty, or sneaking money from someone's pocket. And there's usually always a third wheel here; someone who's left out of all the fun. When this card pops up in a reading, where business or employment are concerned, it's time to bend over and see who's playing under the table with whom.

Page/wands: "Unexpected financial news coming through!", shrieks this card, like one of those old time newspaper hawkers in the 1930's, screaming the headlines. If he's on his feet, the news is good; if he's on his head, you're screwed.

Ace/wands: If you're thinking of starting your own business, changing careers or companies, or in any way starting over where employment and a career are concerned, this is the card you want to see. It's like the green light at a drag race. When you see it, step on the gas, put the pedal to the metal, and roar down the pathway, because it's clear and victory can be yours at the end of the line.

Just remember, once in a while this card turns up reversed, and it says, "Hang on to your hats, it's going to be a bumpy ride." No one ever said that beginnings and change are easy and effortless, and it's this little glitch that usually catches people off guard.

Eight/pentacles: I don't know why, but I always think of the cobbler in that fairy tale whenever I see this card. You know the one, the poor little guy who is working his fingers to the bone repairing shoes and can't keep up with the workload. He goes to sleep one night, dog tired and weary as hell, and something amazing happens. He wakes up to find all of the work finished and rows of sparkling shoes all about his house.

The elves did it.

You can do it too, that's what the eight of pentacles is telling you: learn something new, polish your skills. You haven't reached your full potential…yet.

Two/wands: I hope you have a pen handy. You're going to need it to sign the much anticipated contract that's coming your way. Unlike the three of wands, most of the time things are above board and on the level with the two of wands. Everyone is playing nice and the sandbox is clean.

Money Issues

If it isn't love that people are focused on, it's money. These are the two most important aspects to create a life that's happy and runs smoothly. If there's a problem in either area, it affects everything, like a virus. Money issues are pretty simple really, either you've got it, or you don't.

Ten/pentacles: Yes, this card is all about money, but more than that, it's about the family or group that are involved with the money. That's why I chose to put this card with the others in *Love/Relationships/Family*.

Seven/pentacles: Now we have some money, so what do we do with it? The lackadaisical attitude of this character is one that makes you wonder how he/she ever managed to accumulate any money to begin with. When this card comes up, someone is sitting on the fence where money issues and decisions are concerned. They either seem frozen with fear at the possibility of making a wrong decision, they're just plain lazy, or they have no god-damned idea what it is that they're suppose to do next, not a clue.

The sad thing is, while this individual is stuck in neutral, someone else will come along and mow them down, usually a spouse or business partner, taking off with the coveted prize, that big wad of money that was being so tenderly left to stagnate.

Ace/pentacles: A bird in the hand is worth two in the bush; hold on to what you have; a hand-out; kiss my ass…These are only a few of the impressions left with me by the Ace of pentacles. I suppose I should be all happy and hopeful and grateful when this card comes along. Traditionally it means 'new financial beginnings', tra-la-la. Big fat deal. This card is chintzy. It wants to make you think it's all rich and important and that it's going to be bringing you some tremendous miraculous windfall. It lies.

The Ace of pentacles is just like some sparkling toothy smiling man with a big car and a wad of cash in his pocket. He's never what he seems to be, and he never delivers on anything, including sex, money, or personality.

In the end, it's a big let-down.

Five/pentacles: "They don't have a pot to pee in, or a window to throw it out." This was one of my grandmother's favorite sayings, and it usually depicted a situation in the correct light. So does this card. It's amusing how we love to try and temper this dire financial predicament with the encouraging words, "But this is only a temporary situation." Believe me, there's nothing comforting in that phrase. It's a little hard to be uplifting and to look ahead to the future when your kids are hungry, you had to get rid of the cat or let it starve, you don't know how you're going to pay this month's electric bill, and you have to make excuses when friends invite you out for coffee because, quite frankly, you don't have any money. No, it's the here and now that is your concern. It's getting through the week to next week's paycheck.

This is a shitty card. I don't care how you paint it or attempt to soften it. It still stinks.

Four/pentacles: This is a tight-ass. We've all met one or have had the pleasure or displeasure of their company in some way as a friend, relative, partner, neighbor, business associate.

I've had the distinct misfortune to be married to a tight-ass. I can tell you from observing this type of behavior that the feeling they have for money borders on adoration and worship. It is their god. It is their crack. It is what they live for. They can never have enough of it; they constantly think of ways to make more; they collect piles of it, literally, keeping stacks of coins or paper money stashed away in secret; they spend it pensively, bitter about every penny that slips through their fingers. It really is an addiction, just like any other substance that becomes an obsession.

Every aspect of life can be twisted to revert back to this idol. Often my ex would comment about someone else's wife with a look of absolute horrific disgust on his face, and in a voice dripping with disdain, he would give her the ultimate insult: "She spends *money*."

On September 11th, as we stood ahead of the TV watching a panorama of horror unfold before us, my parents and I held spell bound in disbelief and shock, my ex stood in the center of the room, his arms folded on his chest, stroking his chin in a contemplative way with one hand, and the first comment out of his mouth was: "I bet the stock market will take a dive."

I cringe when I see the four of pentacles.

Nine/pentacles: The nine of pentacles is suppose to be the beautiful lady of leisure, the woman who's either done very well financially on her own, or the pampered Madonna of the upper classes, content in her gilded cage and her very comfortable world.

I don't care how comfortable it is, who in the hell wants to be caged— even if it is gilded.

Case in point:

I meet so many different kinds of people doing tarot readings and some tend to stick with you more than others. This particular woman was one of those.

I met this woman at a shop where I was giving tarot readings. She was probably 10 years or so older than me and had been married to a doctor, but she was divorced now. She sat down for a reading, sliding meekly into a chair across from me, leaning over the table and talking in a conspiratorial manner, looking over her shoulder occasionally, like a child afraid of getting caught doing something they shouldn't be doing. This well-groomed nicely dressed older woman said that she had always attracted 'professional men', and she didn't have anything very flattering to say about her experience. She told me, basically, that they think they are god's gift to the earth; that they make the big money and they know they make the big money, so they expect you to eat out of their hands.

Apparently this woman pretty much did what she was told; whether it be when to go back to work, where to work, how long to work, what she could spend, what she couldn't spend, when she could spend it, ad infinitum. I have never seen a more broken individual in my life. This woman spoke in a subdued whisper, acting as though her great god of an ex-husband might somehow hear what she was saying, the omnipresent ass-hole.

This woman said she had loved sculpture and was just beginning to get the hang of it and to learn, when her husband made her quit sculpting and open a health food store. The store was his idea and she amounted to not much more than unpaid hired help. She worked for nine years in this store she didn't like, in this place she didn't want to be, doing something she didn't want to do— because this man told her she had to.

Thank the goddess, for this woman's sake, her husband eventually found himself another acquiescent baby doll and dumped his aging wife for the new model...a new victim in the making, nice and young and moldable, easy to control.

I'm afraid that this woman's mental health, her emotional state, her own ego and sense of self-worth have been irreparably damaged by this man and her experiences. And of course, she is still under his control, her life still ruled by his decisions, all because of her financial dependence. She told me she has all the material things she wants, nice clothes, beautiful home, jewelry. She has everything but the one thing she desperately longs for...her freedom.

Ladies, there is more to abuse than smacks, snide remarks, or bruises. Exerting extreme and unusual control over another human being is also abuse, and it's the most insidious kind of abuse because it leaves no tell tale marks for friends or family to see.

If you know of a woman who is in an abusive situation, lend her your shoulder, and give her this link...

The National Domestic Abuse Hotline:

As for the nine of pentacles, don't judge the lady on this card until you hear her story. The beautiful golden gilded cage that might look so pretty from the outside may be an absolute frickin' nightmare if you're on the inside looking out.

Six/pentacles: I see someone so loaded with money to the cotton pickin' point where they can throw great armfuls in the air and then lay down on the ground and roll in it. They give to charities, give to friends, give to family. They're always smiling, always friendly, always asking all the polite questions and are excellent with the small talk and mindless chatter, and they are scared to death. They're afraid that someone won't like them. They're afraid of being alone. They're afraid of never finding love or losing friends and family they already have. They think they can be assured of friendship and company in their life by buying it. They live on the surface, afraid to peer below into their own insecurities, hidden agendas, and life traumas.

It's too dark down there.

Another side to the Six of Pentacles:

I see an individual who also has acquired money, enough money to be more than comfortable, enough money to live well and not worry about all the things almost all the rest of us worry about. You know, the little things, those little things that should be taken for granted: the light bill, a movie, gas for the car, treats for the kids, an occasional unexpected shopping adventure, or supper at a favorite restaurant.

This individual, so comfortable in their golden padded little world, watches the people close to them, usually family: children, siblings, aging parents. This individual will watch these people worry and struggle, and they will smile to themselves, an evil little smile like the satisfied smile of a snake before it strikes. This kind of individual will manipulate those close to them by doling out money and helping them out, but there's going to be a price for this, one some of us would think too high to pay. The price is personal freedom, individuality, and independence.

If you stretch out your hand and accept that first golden coin from this benefactor, you will live the rest of your life terrified that you will displease them, that you will fall out of their favor, fall by the wayside, and find yourself once more in a position to worry about all those little things in life and probably a great deal more. By accepting that first golden coin, you are signing away your independence, your individuality, and your self-esteem.

The six of pentacles is a trap.

Two/pentacles: The guy on this card has his hands full. He's the juggler, the distracted individual in the throes of life with more on his plate than is humanly possible to handle, and this includes money and money issues. He spends what he doesn't have and then tries to get through the month to another pay period. Unfortunately, this is the way he handles every other aspect of his life as well, in a helter-skelter mad rush to live, live, live, without planning, without considering the consequences, and without any thought to how he's going to fix things.

The character on the two of pentacles and The Fool must be brothers. They run off down the road on one of life's grand adventures with their heads in the air, no game plan, and no safety net.

Confrontations

The two suits that dominate this category are wands and swords. Wands, associated with the element of Fire, revs up emotions and passions big-time, and not always the good kind. It means hot tempers, sucker punches, fuming, plotting, and straight out attack; it means bickering, belittling, foot stamping, and hissy fits. Swords are more to the point, no pun intended. Just as the sword cuts literally, so does the energy of this suit and these cards. Swords means a shot to the heart, underhanded cowardly attacks, manipulation, and malicious maneuvering; it means wounds fatal to emotional well-being, cruelty, and bullying behavior.

Seven/wands: There's two ways to look at this card. First, is from the character's point of view. This is someone who tends to be extremely paranoid and defensive most of the time, someone who has had to keep their guard up and has probably had to do so for such a long time that it's become second nature. This individual has constructed an emotional wall that many would-be friends, acquaintances, or lovers will be so daunted by that they will eventually give up trying to get through. The result is an individual who carries a chip on their shoulder, a burden that they will find more and more difficult to put down the longer they carry it. Perhaps it is their karma for transgressions from a previous life, or maybe it's their own mental quirk and emotional inconsistency that no one can help or heal. Whatever this demon is, it's inside of them, and only they can cleanse themselves. The secret is that they must want to.

The second way of looking at this card is through a set of circumstances. From this perspective, it represents someone who is being ganged up on by an individual or a group of individuals. Looking at it this way almost always tells us more about the attacker, or attackers, than the victim. Most of the time it's pack animal mentality that comes into play. Think of the movie, "Mean Girls", it exemplifies the bullying aspect of the seven of wands. This card showcases the animal instinct in human beings, the ugly wild "I smell blood and want some" instinct. It reminds me of baby chicks, all fluffy and yellow, adorable and sweet on the outside; but if they smell blood on another chick, those harmless little balls of yellow fluff will gang together and peck their nest mate to a bloody death.

That's what's on the other end of all those wands you see stretched in the air, raised against the character on this card. It's a good thing we can't see the attackers. They would appear frightening, daunting, hateful, spiteful, demonic, ignorant, prejudice, judgmental. Yep, it's a good thing we can't see them. They might look like us.

Five/wands: A group of noisy, out-of-control, bickering, sniveling, hateful, evil little children come to mind. And yes, children can be evil. If you don't believe me, you must not have seen *"Children of the Corn"*. Anyway, that's the attitude that is amplified and carried with this card. This is the worst kind of fight, it's usually over pithy little matters, there's a lot of spite and taking of sides involved, and not surprisingly these sniveling little brats are, in actuality, a pack of immature grownups who have reverted to a second childhood.

My first instinct is to tell them to get over it and grow up already. It's disgusting.

I know a group of adult siblings that perfectly exemplify all the negative qualities of this card. The squabbling in this case usually revolves around:

1) *Parental Favoritism*...Who does Mommy love best? Who's going to win her favor and thus all the perks that go with it; which includes money, vehicles, a loan, a house, ad infinitum. And when you really think about it, is it Mommy they love, or the material possessions that go along with her? This type of behavior also gives Mommy perfect control over her grown children by nurturing unhealthy dependence, often reducing middle-aged adults to petulant five-year-olds, with their hands shoved in their pockets and their eyes on the ground. The rest of the pack all follow Mommy's lead. What else can they do?

2) *Business Entanglements*...The group of squabbling siblings seen on this card don't get along, and yet, how brilliant can this be, they still attempt to do business with each other.

This means lots of sour deals; broken contracts or broken verbal agreements; bitterness; resentment;, cheating; and one-up-manship. Someone always gets left in the mud, usually facedown with someone's footprint on their back.

This is the five of wands.

Nine/wands: Sometimes the character on the nine of wands has a reason for feeling a little defensive and preparing for a fight, and sometimes he doesn't.

When he doesn't, he's wasting his time and energy standing there with a chip on his shoulder waiting for someone to make the first rotten move. This personality takes everything to heart and is so damn hard to talk to because anything you might say could be construed as negative or as a personal attack. The character on this card is usually single or in an unhappy union, spends most of his time in solitary pursuits, rarely smiles, and has that 'hang-dog' look in his eyes. It's the woman you look at and automatically think, 'Bitchy'. This is the energy they radiate, the type of persona they exude.

The other side to this coin, and there's two sides to everything, is that this individual is preparing or should be preparing for an attack, all out war, a gang fight, or at the very least, an unruly mob. Whether this involves their personal life and relationships, or perhaps their employment and the people found there; they need to be ready to defend themselves. Often my clients will already be aware of this, and this card simply reinforces this fact and lets me in on it, or they are totally unaware of it and take this news as a big surprise: "Now, who would want to do that to me...hmmm?"

Stand there in a stupor, and you'll find out.

Five/swords: Often, by the time I see this card, the battle has already been fought, the bloody and dieing are scattered about the battlefield, and the victor is licking his war wounds— usually snickering smugly to himself as he does so.

You have to ask yourself, "Was it really worth it?"

This card points out how draining and destructive this kind of activity, this kind of mentality, and this kind of action can really be. Yes, it's great if you've won, but what did you win? And what if, just what if, the enemy you so gallantly defeated rouses and regroups? What if this is just the first round, the first battle, in what's going to be a long drawn out war? You have to asses whether you have the stamina, the determination, the where-with-all, and sometimes the money, to continue this battle.

Believe it or not, sometimes it's okay to walk away from a fight.

Ten/swords: This is the darkest card of the tarot deck. It is every enemy you've ever had poised behind you, ready to strike. When I see this card, I know that someone is sick, someone is in peril, someone is facing the fight of their life, and once in a while, a very rare while, someone is going to die.

The clique most often used with the ten of swords is, "Look on the bright side, you're as far down as you can get, there's no way to go but up." I don't find much comfort in this clique. It's a little hard to look on the bright side when you, your family, or friends close to you will be facing demons they may not be able to defeat.

There are two significant things about the ten of swords that I can think of. One is the horizon. If you look at the horizon, you'll see that the sun is about to come up. Translated, if you can find the strength to hang on, to fight the illness, to face the enemy, you will see the dawn of day. The other cards found around the ten of swords usually tells us if this is possible, or if this is just wishful thinking.

The second significant thing about the ten of swords is the fact that if the events depicted in the reading have not yet come to pass, this card will serve as a warning. A warning may give you time and the information you need to dodge the bullet.

Card Combinations

Just as thoughts might run rampant, one leading into another, like wet paint running together in a maze of colors, creating new colors along the way; so tarot cards don't always work alone, but each one lends itself to a story that unfolds with the turn of each card, each new lead, each new perception. When this happens, so often it seems, the meanings of the cards transform to the circumstances and the unique individuals that they touch.

1) Let's look at the same card from three different decks:

Nine/cups
Universal Rider/Waite...The Herbal Tarot...
The Goddess Tarot

First we'll look at the similarities: Two things that all of these cards have in common is a complacent figure seated in the foreground and nine golden cups. The nine of cups, no matter what the deck, seems to reek of smugness in a "I-got-what-I wanted-so-fuck-off" kind of way. That doesn't sound flattering, but if it's you this card is coming up for, you won't care, because you won.

9/cups- Rider/Waite: The male figure on this card is seated in a chair, in front of a table containing the nine golden cups, with his arms crossed over his chest, and a sneaky self-satisfied smirk on his face. I can't help but wonder what this guy did to get what he wanted; whatever it was, he obviously enjoyed every minute of it. This character, even though he's in a passive pose, is full of vim and vigor, and he's damn proud of his accomplishments.

The long blue cloth on the table, falling all the way to the floor, seems to be hiding something. Are there skeletons in the closet perhaps, casualties of ambition?

9/cups- The Herbal Tarot: There is the same familiar figure in the center of the card, but this time the character is rather androgynous and is seated on the ground, arms still crossed but resting on the knees in a very relaxed and casual manner. The smile is soft and gentle, as though the rewards stacked in the background were expected, it was just a matter of time. This character is not sitting out in the open, exposed, but rather is surrounded by a flowering vine, giving the impression that the accomplishments on this card came with a minimum of suffering or hard work, it suggests a rather cushioned existence.

The fact that the golden cups are stacked in two rows, one atop the other, tells us that the accomplishments or treasures were collected over a period of time, possibly a gradual transition to success through a series of planned or synchronistic events.

9/cups- The Goddess Tarot: The beautiful female character on this card, with her flowing blond hair and long pink dress, is holding one of the golden cups, which seems to imply that she is quietly and privately savoring her success, rolling a taste of it around in her pretty little mouth like a fine wine. She has her back to us, not giving a rat's ass about what anyone else thinks. She obviously did not work to accomplish what she's accomplished just to receive praise, adoration, or acceptance from anyone. She seems to be oblivious to us voyeurs; in fact, she appears to be in her own little world, and she seems to like it this way.

I've just interpreted the same card, the nine of cups, from three different decks; and I distinctly felt three very different types of energy from each one. In any case, no matter what the characters' attitudes or attributes, they all got what they wanted.

Let's hope it turns out to be what they were expecting.

2) A Lethal Combination: Death/10 of Swords/The Tower

This combination of tarot cards takes my breath away and makes the hair on the back of my neck stand up. It means death—

terrible, sudden, totally unexpected, and often violent. It has very rarely come up in my readings. But when it has, I have never- *never*- told a querent just how ominous this set of cards can be, until one summer.

During the summer I did a reading for a dear friend. We sat at a small cozy table beneath a beautiful maple tree, with the afternoon sun casting sideways rays at our feet. We were laughing and chatting as I laid the cards, animated and happy on this beautiful day. I laid three groups of three cards each. Then I turned the first group of cards...Death, the ten of swords, and the Tower. Conversation abruptly ceased, and our eyes locked across the table. I felt heartsick. My friend also knows the cards, and I knew that she knew. We spoke a single name in unison. We knew who the cards were speaking of, who the cards were calling for. It wasn't my friend these cards were beckoning, but a member of her family, a member of her family much too young to be called by Death. We both knew, and we felt the violence of it, even on this beautiful sunny day.

I hemmed and hawed, turned some of the other cards, but my heart wasn't in the reading; and finally I said, "If there were any group of cards in this deck that would speak of death, it's these cards. And I just don't want to go there."

I swept the pile of cards together, and we sat at the table a while longer, but all the joy had been taken out of the day. About five months later, there was a terrible accident, and my dear friend lost a young member of her family, the person whose name we had spoken together.

3) Ambivalent Cards
Judgment

This card, no matter what deck it's from, always feels 'holier than thou'. It should be called the smug smart ass 'I-told-you-so' card. If anyone has done anything in their life that wasn't the brightest thing to do, I hate to tell you, but this card will come screaming through the deck to tattle on you, just like that kid in grade school that no one could stand. You know the one, the snitch.

In spite of its very dramatic appearance, I give this card as much clout as the crumpled Kleenex in the bottom of my purse. Everyone has done something in their life that's stupid. You can admit it, no one's listening right now. When I turn this card in a reading, I have all I can do not to roll my eyes. Because of it's very dramatic and high fa-lutin symbolism, I suppose I've had more than one querent wonder why I brush it off.

It's because, when I'm reading for you, my concern is on your future and what's going to happen to you from this point on. What are you going to do now, what direction will your life take, and what is your destination? *What you're going to do is much more important to me than what you've done.* I could care less if you screwed the neighbor's wife or cheated on your taxes.

The World

This card gives the impression of running in circles- the card, not the querent. The World, which is often a beautiful card in most decks, leaves an odd taste in my mouth. It's sneaky; and once in a while it feels as though it's trying to slip something tricky into the reading, deliberately trying to throw a wrench in what I see, what I feel, what I know is there. This is one of my least favorite cards, and quite frankly, I've never gotten a good message or omen from it. It must be obvious that I don't care for this tarot card, and I almost feel like I should whisper this revelation, as though the card might be listening and will send down a wave of negative energy to kick my ass.

The Wheel of Fortune

A change of luck, blah, blah, blah. This is so redundant, and it can mean many things, or it can mean nothing, but mostly it wants to give you a shot of artificial hope. The Wheel of Fortune and The World both have one thing in common, the circle. And this card would just love to get you running in circles, all whipped up in a white heat, searching for the elusive idea of instant good fortune and "Lady Luck". In the meantime, if you listen really hard, you can almost hear the characters on this card snickering in devilish delight. It's appearance at a reading almost always inspires a surprised hopeful look from the querent, and so often I've wanted to say, "Don't get your hopes up so fast."

The Wheel of Fortune is often called 'the gambler's card', and it's main purpose is to tell us that life is one big fat frickin' game of chance.

Temperance

In most decks I've seen, the character on this card looks just like the angels that graced the windows in the old Catholic church that was connected to the parochial school I attended as a kid. This card gives me the feeling of aloofness, social snootiness. The angel won't even look us in the eye, pretending to be so intrigued by the chalices and their contents that she's mindlessly pouring back and forth, back and forth. 'If I don't look at them, they'll go away', she thinks. Quite frankly, and I've never told a querent this, but sometimes this card shows up simply to point out how boring someone is or how mundane their circumstances. This card most often just wants to tell us what a stinking rut our lives are in, how stuck we are by circumstances of our own making, and how goddamn boring we can really be.

4) Who's Who?—Court Card Personality Types[22]

For a look at the softer side of the court cards, refer to the section of this book titled, **Your Tarot Journal**.

Each court card represents archetypical energy. Each court card also represents a personality type, and when someone comes for a reading, it's generally to uncover those things about other personalities that may be on the negative side. This fact might dismay some people, but it's the truth. No one feels the need to uncover more information about an individual who is not having a negative impact on their existence. We don't need more insight into someone who is loving, cheerful, agreeable, and sweet. We need more insight into the bastard who's screwing up our life.

Kings: Exposing the Male Persona

King of Pentacles...This guy is all about money and control, and he has a real talent and knack for using the two together to rigidly control and manipulate other people's lives in an utterly ruthless calculating way. And if he's really- *really*- good at it, he'll find a way to carry this tradition on long after he's dead and buried. He might make a good mob boss, but he has this penchant about following the rules and obeying laws, at least most of the time, as long as he can make sure that he'll get his way in the end. He is cold-hearted, cruel, calculating, blood-thirsty, and highly sexual. He wants what he wants when he wants it, whatever it is. The King of pentacles sees the world as either black or white. Translated, this means that you are either with him or against him. This skewered view of the world and relationships often makes him appear paranoid, and if you don't share his skewered view of the world, you will never gain access to his sacred inner sanctum.

King of Swords...This character's biggest enemies are his mouth and his ego, and they tend to run together- on and on and on and on. He doesn't know when to shut up, and this is because he's too busy 'enlightening' the rest of the world, all of whom are much less intelligent than yours truly. His opinions are not set in stone, they're set in gold, and he expects the rest of the world to embrace them with open-mouthed awe-struck enthusiasm. This guy is loud and in your face. The one weird quirk here is that you'd think he might be crude, but no, this King runs in the other direction. He tends to be overly prudish, to the point of some pretty kinky extremes. Let's just say he might have 'issues'.

King of Wands...This King is also about control, but this King is also a coward, a coward and a bully. He'll control those around him in whining, backstabbing, petty, hurtful ways. He lives in a world of his own reality. Tell him how you honestly feel about any issue, including him, and he'll deny it. Tell him that the sky is blue, and he'll argue the subject. He will have one thing that he worships to the point of obsession. He will adore his obsession. He will collect it, look at it, sort it, hide it; he will take it out from time to time to revel in it. This obsession, whatever it is, will take precedence over the feelings of those close to him, or the well being of family. This guy is also ruthlessly rigid and conservative in his behavior, generally closely tied to a religious belief system, usually whatever he was raised in and is familiar with. He tends to take his religious fanaticism to extremes. He's the guy who will screw his wife but only on Sundays and usually with the lights off.

King of Cups...This character is smooth, really smooth, he can tell you anything in a way that will make you believe it. He'll also screw anything he can get his hands on with nary a qualm of conscience to the act. He is the epitome of hedonism. He will indulge in not only sex, but food and drink, and anything else he has a penchant for. This guy also tends to be lazy, so you won't find him with a long list of impressive accomplishments. His main goal in life is to 'eat, drink, and be merry', and he excels at all three. He may seem laid back and easy going, but if you cross him, you will discover that he's childish and tends to be passive aggressive. If you've pissed him off, you may not know it until you find a very expensive pair of your shoes planted upside down in the garden.

Queens: The Bitch in Us All

Queen of Pentacles...Oh, my gawds. This woman is all mouth, and it's usually wide open with opinions and judgments rolling through like a dam that's burst. Ignoring her won't do any good, she'll keep asking the same personal obnoxious questions over and over. The fact that you're trying to ignore her bad behavior will never occur to her. If you think she likes you, you'd better think again, after you've heard what she's had to say behind your back. This gal tends to be very vain, and in her younger years she may very well have been quite attractive. She doesn't want anyone to forget this. She also tends to be very promiscuous in early life and probably screwed half her high school class, or half the married men in town.

Queen of Swords...This Queen is the classical 'Bitch', with a capitol B. She's got a tongue in her mouth that could cut the strongest most stalwart man in half. She is cold, calculating, unfortunately intelligent enough to put together great 'get even' schemes, and ruthless enough to pull them off without batting an eye. This character is as cold as the iceberg that sunk the Titanic, and she's usually frigid. This Queen thinks very highly of herself and will most likely remain single, or at least remain single until later in life. This is because, when you're damn near perfect, it's difficult to find anyone who's worthy of your presence.

Queen of Wands...If this Queen can't control it, whether it be people or circumstances, she will bend it, twist it, torture it, or beat it into submission until she can. Her gift is the ability to give anyone she disapproves of the cold shoulder, and she's marvelously talented at this. She can ignore someone she views as an adversary, and this includes anyone not willing to kiss her ass, to the point where they might begin wonder if they really are invisible. This is because all of her minions will follow suit, ignoring the black sheep right along with this Queen. If they don't, they know they'll wind up on her shit list, right along with the poor bastard who just happens to be her 'Target of the Moment'.

Queen of Cups...This Queen's biggest fear is that someone won't like her. She will bend over backwards to appear as something different to each individual she associates with. If the person she's talking to likes horses, she'll be a horsewoman; if the person she's talking to is a right-wing Christian conservative, her great-grandmother on her father's side was Baptist. If the person she's talking to likes seafood, so does she. Because of this crazy idea that she has to be all to everyone and that everyone *must* like her, she's also a slut, not because she's fantastically sexual and earthy, but because she's afraid that if she says 'no', the guy will not like her, and he'll never call again. So she screws him even though she may know better, and then wonders why he never calls again. In reality, she's not looking for sex. She's looking for love and approval. The Queen of Cups is the most pathetic of the Queens.

Knights: Wild Boys

Knight of Pentacles...This character is a younger version of the King of Pentacles. He's immature yet, still learning how to be all cut-throat and cutting edge, taking in all the highs and lows of money matters and the art of manipulation. In the meantime, he gives the impression of being the solid, safe, silent type. This is because his young brain is quietly taking life in, honing the blade for future conquests, building the foundation of his dynasty, deciding whose going to ascend the ladder with him and who he'll bury under the bottom rung. And if you think he's the strong silent type, piss him off and watch the tantrum unfold. This Knight can pitch a fit like no other; he's got foot stamping down to an art.

Knight of Swords...This card typifies the asshole, with a capitol

A. His mouth runs on its own, with no thought or consideration to any pain or damage that his young tongue might cause along the way. He's practicing for when he gets all grown up and knows everything about everything, and everyone will ask for his expert opinion. In the meantime, he's putting a new definition to the word 'obnoxious', and he's grooming himself for the position he feels life has in store for him. You can try to ignore him, but it won't do much good. If you don't give him the response he expects, he figures that you must not have heard him, and he'll just repeat his sarcastic comment, only *louder*.

Knight of Wands...He looks like 'the good boy', standing quietly in the midst of life's foray, chewing his fingernails, head lowered, eyes shifting back and forth to take in the scene, trying to decide who'd be the easiest target to control. Who would he be able to bluff and bully without revealing his own weaknesses? 'Good boy', my ass. This character has his life charted and planned out from day one, and anyone who comes into this life better fit to all the pegs and holes, or he'll chop off whatever doesn't, trying to ram everything and everyone into perfect order. He tends to be neurotic and self-righteous enough to make you vomit. He sees something wrong with everyone but himself.

Knight of Cups...This character is the reason chastity belts were invented. He sees every woman as a conquest and measures every woman he sees to his own yardstick of beauty, which can be pretty idealistic. At this stage of life, he might have some pretty big plans for his future, but don't worry, nothing will actually materialize. He'll use up all his energy to satisfy his physical needs; and considering that the seeds of laziness have already been planted, watered, and fertilized, big plans will come to naught. Besides, just when he's conquered one woman, a prettier one will come along, and off he runs.

Pages: Youth is Wasted on the Young

Page of Pentacles...This guy is sullen, quiet, and moody; he'll push boundaries to the limit and may find himself in a pack of trouble because of this bent. Just because he doesn't say anything outwardly negative to you, don't think he really likes you, he just knows how to keep disdain simmering low on the back burner. This Page also tends to be good-looking, and this fact contributes to his penchant for getting away with murder. We're more likely to let a pretty boy off the hook. This character could go any which way in later life. Either he'll straighten himself out and discover the wondrous world of the adult, embracing all the responsibilities that go along with it; or he'll wind up living in a cardboard box in some back alley, swigging cheap wine for breakfast. It's his call.

Page of Swords...This Page is a bitch in the making. He/she is a younger version of the King or Queen of swords. It's already difficult carrying on a conversation with this Page, because everything is all about them; it's the only topic they care to discuss. They're conversation is blunt, verging on rude. Vanity is already at work here, and because of their youth and immaturity, it can actually get to the point of ridiculous. They have a skewered view of how attractive they really are, or how accomplished, how smart, etc. Even now, and very sadly, they are setting a solitary path for themselves by alienating people who may actually love them. They treat people like shit, and then act all puzzled when friends and acquaintances disappear.

Page of Wands...This Page tends to be nothing more than a milder version of the Page of Swords. Think of this character as a Valley Girl gone Goth. The mouth keeps running, and running, and running; unfortunately, the brain hasn't caught up. They are only able to maintain successful relationships for a limited length of time, until the persona they are trying to portray evaporates and their real personality slips out...oops. There's no getting around the fact that the Page of Wands has a mean streak. This Page has a very short attention span, and this unfortunately includes such things as an interest in pets and people. If you know a Page of Wands who has a dog or cat, the odds are they're going to dump this critter off on you when their enthusiasm begins to wane. The one bright spot for this Page is a very strong work ethic and a dedication to their job. Where this comes from, go figure.

Page of Cups...This young Page is super sensitive, and it means that you might find yourself walking on eggshells in order not to offend the young Prince/Princess. However, if you do tick him/her off, you might want to stand back to watch the hissy fit and keep yourself safe from the fallout. With that said, this is still the most affable of all the Pages, with the most promise of being 'normal', whatever normal is. One of the biggest problems is that this character has a habit of setting unrealistic goals for her/himself and then practically killing themselves trying to live up to these idealistic endeavors. Nothing is ever good enough, big enough, expensive enough, fancy enough, or just plain 'enough'. This Page develops strong ties to people and places, and you'll find that the relationships/friendships that they cultivate early in life will last for decades.

Traditional Meanings:
Because We Have To

Okay, I surrender. I'll post the traditional meanings for the cards Ace-ten for all four suits, short and sweet and to the point. But I won't post traditional meanings for the court cards because, quite frankly, there's nothing 'traditional' about them; and if you keep doing readings long enough, you'll come to realize this too. I did, however, post a softer side to these characters in the section of this book called, *"Your Tarot Journal"*.

Minor Arcana
Pentacles

Ace: Beginnings...money, prosperity, material gain
Two: Balance
Three: Celebration
Four: Miserliness
Five: Poverty
Six: Prosperity
Seven: Hoarding
Eight: Apprenticeship
Nine: Wealth, accomplishment, satisfaction
Ten: Inheritance, group money issues

Swords

Ace: Beginnings...mental endeavors, creative projects
Two: Crossroads, standoff
Three: Heartache
Four: Illness, rest/recuperation
Five: Battle
Six: Movement
Seven: Thievery
Eight: Feeling trapped
Nine: Nightmares, stress
Ten: Treachery

Wands

Ace: Beginnings...financial matters, business
Two: Partnership
Three: Success
Four: Stability
Five: Disagreement
Six: Victory
Seven: Defense

Eight: Movement
Nine: Battle ready
Ten: Burdens

Cups

Ace: Beginnings...relationships
Two: Couples
Three: Celebration
Four: Deliberation
Five: Mourning
Six: Your past
Seven: Decisions
Eight: Abandonment
Nine: Wish card
Ten: Successful home-life

The Major Arcana:
Life in a Shot Glass

0 The Fool: Road sign..."Idiot's Cross Here"...drive slowly.

1 The Magician: The hand is quicker than the eye.

2 The High Priestess: Use your fricken' head!

3 The Empress: Life is preggers.

4 The Emperor: All man, and don't you forget it.

5 The Hierophant: Get a life, for Christ's sake.

6 The Lovers: Hooking up.

7 The Chariot: Run baby, and don't look back.

8 Strength: Get a spine.

9 The Hermit: "I 'vant to be alone." (Greta Garbo)

10 Wheel of Fortune: Don't bet on it.

11 Justice: Holier than thou.

12 The Hanged Man: Pity party.

13 Death: Your mother warned you, and you didn't listen.

14 Temperance: How dull can it be?

15 The Devil: What you do when no one's looking.

16 The Tower: Shit happens.

17 The Star: The glass is half full, if you squint.

18 The Moon: Liar, liar, pants on fire.

19 The Sun: Everybody smile...say 'cheese'.

20 Judgment: I told you so.

21 The World: What goes around comes around.

Connecting with the Tarot

The four suits of the tarot deck: pentacles, swords, wands, cups, and their court cards (Kings, Queens, Knights, and Pages) correspond with the suits found in a regular deck of playing cards. Did you realize that a regular deck of playing cards can be used for divination?

The suits will correspond as so:

pentacles/spades

swords/diamonds

wands/clubs

hearts/cups

Of course, a regular deck of playing cards will lack the 22 cards that make up the major arcana, the big picture; but you'll still get an in-depth look at all the small and intricate twists and turns of life.

Minor Arcana Connections
By the Number

Ace: *Beginnings-* fresh ideas, new growth, opportunities, challenges, new energy or a renewal of energy

Two: *Decisions-* duality, balance or imbalance, relationships, partnerships, couples, acknowledgment

Three: *Growth-* celebration, growth through partnerships and connections, discovery, karmic lessons

Four: *Foundations-* facing responsibilities, maturity, material issues, understanding through emotional growth

Five: *Change-* challenges, disappointments, gaining strength through adversity, overcoming obstacles

Six: *Stability-* success, peace, values, recognition, ancestral connections, wisdom

Seven: *Limits-* learning through deception, fate, choices, evolutions, completions through trial and error

Eight: *Infinity-* control, growth through spirituality, expansion through experimentation

Nine: *Reassessment-* facing our own demons, coming to terms, wisdom, the psyche

Ten: *Completion-* the end of a cycle, success, perfection, nirvana, lessons learned

The Suits
Pentacles

Element: Earth
Zodiac: Capricorn, Taurus, Virgo
Stone: brown jasper, aventurine, jade, hematite
Season: winter
Ace: herb/whole grains
2: planet/Jupiter; zodiac/Capricorn; herb/yellow dock
3: planet/Mars; zodiac/Capricorn; herb/gentian
4: planet/Sun; zodiac/Capricorn; herb/cascara bark
5: planet/Mercury; zodiac/Taurus; herb/mugwort
6: planet/Moon; zodiac/Taurus; herb/hops
7: planet/Saturn; zodiac/Taurus; herb/rhubarb
8: planet/Sun/; zodiac/Virgo; herb/ginger
9: planet/Venus; zodiac/Virgo; herb/dark grapes
10: planet/Mercury; zodiac/Virgo; herb/wild yams

Swords

Element: Air
Zodiac: Libra, Aquarius, Gemini
Stone: amber, citrine, topaz, zircon

Season: Spring

Ace: herb/chamomile
2: planet/Moon; zodiac/Libra; herb/passionflower
3: planet/Saturn; zodiac/Libra; herb/pleurisy root
4: planet/Jupiter; zodiac/Libra; herb/mullein
5: planet/Venus; zodiac/Aquarius; herb/mistletoe
6: planet/Mercury; zodiac/Aquarius; herb/vervain
7: planet/Moon; zodiac/Aquarius; herb/wood betony
8: planet/Jupiter; zodiac/Gemini; herb/black cohash
9: planet/Mars; zodiac/Gemini; herb/valerian
10: planet/Sun; zodiac/Gemini; herb/ephedra

Wands

Element: Fire
Zodiac: Aries, Leo, Sagittarius
Stone: carnelian, ruby, garnet, fire opal
Season: Summer

Ace: herb/yarrow
2: planet/Mars; zodiac/Aries; herb/basil
3: planet/Sun; zodiac/Aries; herb/saffron
4: planet/Venus; zodiac/Aries; herb/fennel seed
5: planet/Saturn; zodiac/Leo; herb/turmeric
6: planet/Jupiter; zodiac/Leo; herb/hawthorn
7: planet/Mars; zodiac/Leo; herb/wild ginger
8: planet/Mercury; zodiac/Sagittarius; herb/sassafras
9: planet/Moon; zodiac/Sagittarius; herb/bayberry bark
10: planet/Saturn; zodiac/Sagittarius; herb/prickly ash bark

Cups

Element: Water
Zodiac: Cancer, Scorpio, Pisces
Stone: blue sapphire, lapis lazuli, amethyst, moonstone

Season: autumn

Ace: herb/lotus
2: planet/Venus; zodiac/Cancer; herb/uva ursi[33] Warning: uva ursi is toxic and can cause serious liver damage if ingested.
3: planet/Mercury; zodiac/Cancer; herb/trillium
4: planet/Moon; zodiac/Cancer; herb/burdock
5: planet/Mars; zodiac/Scorpio; herb/horse tail
6: planet/Sun; zodiac/Scorpio; herb/watermelon
7: planet/Venus; zodiac/Scorpio; herb/juniper berries
8: planet/Saturn; zodiac/Pisces; herb/gravel root
9: planet/Jupiter; zodiac/Pisces; herb/squaw vine
10: planet/Mars; zodiac/Pisces; herb/marijuana

The Court Card Connections
Pentacles

King: herb/alphalpha; zodiac/Taurus
Queen: herb/marshmallow; zodiac/Capricorn
Knight: herb/elecampane; zodiac/Virgo
Page: herb/blue flag

Swords

King: herb/St. John's Wort; zodiac/Aquarius
Queen: herb/lady's slipper; zodiac/Libra
Knight: herb/wild cherry; zodiac/Gemini
Page: herb/dill

Wands

King: herb/cinnamon; zodiac/Leo
Queen: herb/raspberry; zodiac/Aries
Knight: herb/aconite; zodiac/Sagittarius
Page: herb/shepherd's purse

Cups

King: herb/saw palmetto; zodiac/Scorpio
Queen: herb/lady's mantle; zodiac/Cancer
Knight: herb/sarsaparilla; zodiac/Pisces
Page: herb/damiana

Major Arcana Connections
The Fool

Zodiac: Aries
Planet: Uranus
Hebrew Letter: Aleph
Number: 0
Element: Air
Deities: the God, Morpheus
Stones: emerald, Rhine pebble stone
Herbs: lemon balm
Sepher Yetzirah[44] Sepher Yetzirah: "Book of Formation," or "Book of Creation," is the title of the earliest extant book on Jewish esotericism.
Breath of Life, Spirit
Key Words: journey; beginnings; adventure; the unknown; traveling; life quest; look before you leap; optimism; spontaneity, innocence, naiveté

The Magician

Zodiac: Aries
Planet: Mercury
Hebrew Letter: Bet
Number: 1
Element: Air
Deities: Hermes Trigmegistus, Thoth, Hanuman
Stones: diamond, pyrite
Herbs: bayberry, ginseng, nutmeg (flower)
Sepher Yetzirah: Attention, life and death
Key Words: power; magic; the elements- earth, air, fire, water;

the impossible; the occult, infinity; ritual; retaining or reclaiming control; mastery; accomplishment

The High Priestess

Zodiac: Taurus
Planet: Venus
Hebrew Letter: Gimel
Number: 6
Element: Earth
Deities: the Goddess in her aspect of Mother or Creatrix
Stones: chalcedony, serpentine
Herbs: cloves
Sepher Yetzirah: Memory, peace and strife
Key Words: feminine spirituality; the feminine divine; occult mysteries; intuition; the goddess; acquiring knowledge; wisdom; foresight

The Empress

Zodiac: Taurus
Planet: Venus
Hebrew Letter: Dalet
Number: 3
Element: Earth
Deities: Great Mother Goddess
Stones: jasper, carnelian, rose quartz
Herbs: rose, sandalwood, clary sage
Sepher Yetzirah: Imagination, wisdom and folly
Key Words: fertility; feminine issues; the feminine mystique; physical wealth; growth; abundance; nature

The Emperor

Zodiac: Aries

Planet: Mars
Hebrew Letter: Heh
Number: 9
Element: Fire
Deities: Jahwe, Wotan, Zeus
Stones: black onyx, rock crystal
Herbs: ironwood, wormwood, eucalyptus
Sepher Yetzirah: Reason, sight
Key Words: strength; men's issues; masculine energy; force-fulness; fortitude; maintaining control; ancestry

The Hierophant

Zodiac: Taurus
Planet: Earth
Hebrew Letter: Vau
Number: 5
Element: Earth
Deities: the God in all three aspects, the Christian trinity
Stones: amethyst, orange zircon
Herbs: frankincense
Sepher Yetzirah: Intuition, hearing
Key Words: traditionalism; conservatism; religion; spirituality; spirituality put to the test; intolerance; prejudice; strict formality; rigidness

The Lovers

Zodiac: Cancer
Planet: Mercury
Hebrew Letter: Zain
Number: 5
Element: Air
Deities: Feminine- Aphrodite, Inanna, Venus; masculine-Eros, Amor
Stones: carnelian, red coral, rose quartz

Herbs: musk, sandalwood
Sepher Yetzirah: Discrimination, smell
Key Words: physical attraction; true love; soul mates; sexuality; liberation; freedom of expression; free spirit

The Chariot

Zodiac: Cancer
Planet: Moon
Hebrew Letter: Chet
Number: 2
Element: Water
Deities: Shiva, Osiris
Stones: garnet, star sapphire
Herbs: cedar, cypress, cardamom
Sepher Yetzirah: Receptive will, speech
Key Words: movement; travel; modes of transportation; inner journeys; choices; diverse paths; steering one's own life course

Justice

Zodiac: Libra
Planet: Venus
Hebrew Letter: Lamed
Number: 6
Element: Air
Deities: Pallas Athena, Rhea Dictynna, Libera, Maat
Stones: blue sapphire
Herbs: lilies
Sepher Yetzirah: Equilibrium, action, work
Key Words: the judicial system; fairness; playing fair; skepticism; balance/imbalance; legal issues; legal papers, contracts; chivalry

The Hermit

Zodiac: Virgo
Planet: Mercury
Hebrew Letter: Yod
Number: 5
Element: Earth
Deities: Cronos, Hermes
Stones: onyx, crystal
Herbs: juniper, frankincense, wormwood
Sepher Yetzirah: Response and union of opposites, touch
Key Words: solitude; loneliness; privacy; withdrawing; skepticism; mistrust; soul searching; spiritual journeys; peace

Wheel of fortune

Zodiac: Aquarius
Planet: Jupiter
Hebrew letter: Koph
Number: 1
Element: Earth
Deities: Fortuna, Nornes of Fate
Stones: fluorite
Herbs: mugwort, hyssop
Sepher Yetzirah: Rotation, wealth and poverty
Key Words: Lady Luck, success, change of circumstances, completion, coming full circle, indecision, running in circles

Strength

Zodiac: Leo
Planet: Sun
Hebrew Letter: Tet
Number: 1
Element: Fire

Deities: Anuket, Hebe, Cyrene
Stones: ruby
Herbs: neroli, patchouli, niaouli
Sepher Yetzirah: Suggestion, digestion
Key Words: dominance; domination; overpowering the enemy; overcoming obstacles; maintaining control; being in charge; strength of will

The Hanged Man

Zodiac: Pisces
Planet: Neptune
Hebrew Letter: Mem
Number: 3
Element: Water
Deities: Odin, Prometheus, Attis, Schemchasai
Stones: topaz (colorless), turquois (green-blue), calamine
Herbs: garlic, onion, valerian
Sepher Yetzirah: Reversal, suspended mind
Key Words: self-sacrifice; martyrdom; self-esteem issues; paranoia; spirituality in a twisted version; relinquishing control; indecision

Death

Zodiac: Scorpio
Planet: Mars/Pluto
Hebrew Letter: Nun
Number: 9
Element: Water
Deities: Hades, Thanatos, Hypnos, Nyx
Stones: malachite, onyx, nephrite
Herbs: mushrooms
Sepher Yetzirah: Transformation, motion
Key Words: transition; ethereal planes; deterioration; hesitation; the grim reaper; personal fears; negative

influence

Temperance

Zodiac: Sagittarius
Planet: Jupiter
Hebrew Letter: Samekh
Number: 3
Element: Fire
Deities: Isis, Nemesis
Stones: yellow sapphire, gold topaz
Herbs: lavender, goldenrod
Sepher Yetzirah: Verification, wrath
Key Words: balance; stability; spiritual profoundness; calmness; tenacity in the face of adversity; angels...and daemons

The Devil

Zodiac: Capricorn
Planet: Saturn
Hebrew Letter: Ayin
Number: 8
Element: Earth
Deities: Lucifer, Seth, Baal, Pan
Stones: fire opal, almandite
Herbs: tobacco, sulphur
Sepher Yetzirah: Bondage, mirth
Key Words: the dark side; obsessions, compulsions, addictions; the weak link; inner demons; and daemons

The Tower

Zodiac: Sagittarius
Planet: Mars
Hebrew Letter: Peh
Number: 7

Element: Fire
Deities: Shiva, Zeus, Thor
Stones: malachite, black opal
Herbs: hemlock, calamus root
Sepher Yetzirah: Awakening, grace and sin
Key Words: chaos; catastrophe; carnage; unexpected assault or attack; devastation; complete transformation; clearing the debris

The Star

Zodiac: Aquarius
Planet: Uranus
Hebrew Letter: Tzaddi
Number: 4
Element: Air
Deities: Astarte, Isis, Ischtar, seven priestesses of the oracle
Stones: aquamarine, rose quartz, star sapphire, lapis lazuli
Herbs: jasmine, rose, ophire, almond oil
Sepher Yetzirah: Revelation, meditation
Key Words: unbridled hope; optimism; the light at the end of the tunnel; personal revelations; infinity; the dreamscape

The Moon

Zodiac: Pisces
Planet: Neptune
Hebrew Letter: Qof
Number: 7
Element: Water
Deities: Anubis, Khephra, Hecate, Medusa, Hydra, Kali
Stones: water opal, moonstone
Herbs: mint, coca, peyote, poppy seeds
Sepher Yetzirah: Organization, sleep
Key Words: magic; deception; dark revelations; feminine spirituality; occult mysticism; estrangement; secrets

The Sun

Zodiac: Leo
Planet: Sun
Hebrew Letter: Resh
Number: 1
Element: Fire
Deities: Apollo, Helios, Hyperion, Huitzilopochtli, Krishna, Papa Legba, Lug, Ra Rama, Semesh, Sol, Vishnu
Stones: diamond
Herbs: bay leaf
Sepher Yetzirah: Regeneration, sterility and fertility
Key Words: happiness; deep seated contentment; brilliance of thought; complacency; individualism; courage

Judgment

Zodiac: Aquarius
Planet: Pluto
Hebrew Letter: Shin
Number: 2
Element: Fire
Deities: The Messiah
Stones: zircon (orange)
Herbs: myrrh
Sepher Yetzirah: Realization, decision
Key Words: intolerance; snobbishness; degradation; setting limits; accepting the consequences of your actions; conservative thinking

The World

Zodiac: Scorpio
Planet: Saturn
Hebrew Letter: Taw
Number: 3
Element: Air

Deities: The All, the Source

Stones: fluorite (clear), clear quartz crystals

Herbs: lavender, moon flower, mugwort

Sepher Yetzirah: Universal consciousness, dominion and slavery

Key Words: completion; the end; starting over; finishing up; reaching a goal; full potential; running in circles

Major Arcana and the Runes

Runes are the magical alphabet of northern and central Europe. Although they were used for writing, the runes were primarily used for divination. They are considered sacred signs, symbols that have the ability to connect you with your past, your ancestors, and the spirit world.

Fehu: The Tower

Uruz: High Priestess

Thurisaz: The Emperor

Ansuz: Death

Raidho: Hierophant

Kenaz: Chariot

Gebo: The Lovers

Wunjo: Strength

Hagalaz: The World

Nauthiz: The Devil

Isa: The Hermit

Jera: The Fool

Eihwaz: Hanged Man

Perthro: Wheel of Fortune

Algiz: Moon

Sowilo: The Sun

Tiwaz: Justice

Berkano: The Empress

Ehwaz: The Lovers

Mannaz: The Magician
Laguz: The Star
Ingwaz: Judgment
Dagaz: Temperance
Othala: The Moon

Tarot Spreads

A *lot* of importance sometimes seems to be placed on *tarot spreads*, the pattern in which the cards are laid out for a reading. Each position is generally given a very specific meaning, and the card that winds up in this position is usually read with this direction in mind. This does work, and it can be amazing when the reading all comes together. However, we have to be careful not to put so much emphasis and importance on the position in a tarot spread and what it represents that we miss what the card is trying to tell us.

I will always remember watching a professional psychic working with members of a police department, trying to give them information to solve a criminal case. This woman was using an oversized Thoth deck. The cards were battered and beaten, ragged eared and wonderful. With no pomp or preparation, she quickly spread out a small silk scarf on the table before her. Holding the large deck in her left hand, she lowered her head and began turning card after card after card. This woman laid each card she drew in a single pile on the scarf, commenting now and then, giving an impression, a feeling, a color, a direction, an eerie insight, a quick view inside the mind of the criminal and the world of his victim. There was no spread used, just the cards and this woman's natural incredible intuition.

No matter what spread you use, if the card you see before you has a different message than what is expected of it, listen. Don't dismiss it. With that said, we're going to enjoy and delve into a variety of tarot spreads and find out how they can be used to answer very specific questions. These tarot spreads are both spreads I've developed for myself and have used successfully over the years, as well as new spreads I've created specifically for this book. These are spreads created for the reader who wants to read for him/herself; and yes, you can do this. Some people will be more successful at it than others, but it can be done.

This is my book, my tarot, it's written the way I personally use the cards. And I want to state right now that the *pattern* in which you lay the cards out is totally irrelevant to my readings, it's the *intent* for which each card is laid out that is of supreme importance. I have one exception to this preference, and that would be what I call the "Pyramid Window". You'll learn more about that in this section.

Romance Spreads

Readings dealing with romance and love take precedence over all other readings, even money, especially money. It seems that if your love life is complicated or simply not working, everything else in life slides into the background. Some people, totally absorbed in the question of love, barely seem to function in the real world, so obsessed they are with the questions they have…Does he really love me? Is he cheating? Will he marry me? When will he marry me? Will he stay? Will he leave? Will I ever find true love?

Romance can be an obsession, like a drug. And more often than not, we'll turn to the cards for the answers we must have in order to be able to return our lives to some semblance of normalcy.

1. Is he cheating?

This is one of the most intense questions that arises for relationship readings. Quite frankly, I feel that probably 90% of the people who ask me this question already know the answer, they are just looking to have it validated.

1) Lay three cards representing the man.

These cards should reveal a lot about him, both things you already know, as well as new insights into his personality, his behavior, what's important to him, and any skeletons in his closet.

2) Lay three cards to represent you.

This is where it gets tricky, especially when you're reading for yourself. We don't always want an up-close personal look at our own psyche, our own motives, our own behavior. Sometimes we have ulterior motives, we just won't admit it, even to ourselves. The idea here will be to look at these cards objectively and be honest with yourself.

3) Lay three cards to represent the truth.

You might like what you see here, or you might not. If you like it, rejoice; if you don't like it, don't sugar-coat it.

4) What do you really want?
Lay three cards.

This might seem like a strange question, but so often, on deeper reflection, we realize that we don't want we thought we did. Don't become so addicted to fairy tale endings that you feel obligated to chase a dream that might wind up to be a nightmare.

5) The final outcome.
Lay three cards.

This will be the end of the story, or the beginning of it.

2. Eenie, meenie, minie, mo...Which mate for me?

There are people out there, usually adventurous, carefree, self-assured, and flamboyant people who are not afraid to experiment with love. They try a little bit of this and a little bit of that, and they have no qualms about dating more than one person at a time. But eventually, when cupid comes knocking on the door, or their biological clock starts ticking so loudly they can no longer ignore it, these people will want to choose a mate. The problem is, which one to choose.

1) Lay three cards for each suitor.
Remember, the pattern in which you lay the cards out is not the important point here, it's the intention for which you lay out each card. As you're laying cards for each individual, concentrate on this person, visualize them in your mind. See their face, hear their voice, smell their scent.

Lay these cards face up right off the bat. You want an up close and personal look at these individuals, and this includes all the character traits and real feelings that they might not be sharing with you. Are you surprised by what you see? What do you like about each individual, and what do you dislike about them? Are you reassured by what you see, or do the cards raise more questions?

2) For each suitor, you will lay one card that represents your feelings for that individual.
This is where some of you doing this reading might find a surprise or two. Some of you might be reassured by a validation, and for others, you might discover new revelations that change the whole landscape of this scenario.

3) The final outcome.
Lay three cards.
This reminds me of that game show, Let's Make a Deal, remember? What's behind curtain number two? But there was a hitch to this game, a way out, a way to save face. At the end of the show, if you didn't like what you got, you had the option of turning it in for another chance, another curtain to choose from, another door to open.

Whatever the outcome, don't allow yourself to be trapped by circumstances or expectations in a situation you still may have doubts about, or with a lover that leaves you questioning your choice.

3. Will he marry me?

This is the million dollar question. Women seem transfixed, mesmerized, obsessed, and insane when it comes to this topic. They will bend over backwards to flatter, to please, to change themselves to meet the needs of the man they have targeted. Some of these women don't even realize that this is what they've done, targeted someone, but that's pretty much what it boils down to. This instinct runs deep through the blood and the subconscious, it crosses cultural boundaries and assassinates common sense and any thoughts of independence. It rules the lives of girl children from the time they are old enough to be hypnotized and cultified by the likes of Snow White and Cinderella.

Sad, but true.

The easiest no nonsense way to ask this question is to cut to the chase and seek a direct yes/no answer. *Before* you ask the question, you will determine which cards in the tarot deck represent 'yes', and which cards in the tarot deck represent 'no'.

I've made it easy for you:[55] You might want to bookmark this page. You're going to be referring back to this section for future yes/no questions.

The Suits 2-10: even numbers 'yes'; odd numbers 'no'.

Aces: cups & wands, yes; swords & pentacles, no.

The Court Cards: Kings, no; Queens, yes; Knights- cups & wands, yes; swords & pentacles, no; Pages- cups & wands, yes; swords & pentacles, no.

Major Arcana: even numbered cards, yes; odd numbered cards, no.

4. Will I find true love?

1) Lay a card to signify you, a card that you have chosen specifically.
This is usually a court card, one of the personality prototypes, but it doesn't necessarily have to be. I talked with a lady once who considered the major arcana card 'The Star' her significator.

2) Across this card— face down— lay a card to represent the final outcome.
Don't look at this card yet. You have other things to consider before you face the final answer to this question.

3) Lay three cards to represent your personal goals for the future.
Lay these cards face up right away. Even though you think you know what your goals are, you might be surprised at how enlightening the cards can be. Sometimes we have goals that we feel are so over the top, so out of reach, that we shove them to the back of our subconscious. It's easier to pack them away than to face the challenge of meeting them and getting off our ass, stretching ourselves past our limits, and working to reach a dream we labeled as impossible.

4) Lay three cards to represent what attributes you seek in a mate.
Just exactly what are you looking for in your future lover and companion? Besides the obvious and clique- tall, dark, handsome, curvy, intelligent, caring, blah, blah, blah- the unexpected will pop up; and it will pop up in the form of person-ality traits, quirks, and characteristics that you maybe wouldn't admit you're looking for or you are not even consciously aware of. Lay these cards face up right away too, you might as well look your future lover in the eye. And, by the way, do you recognize this individual? The character that you see depicted in these three cards may very well be someone you already know.

5) Now turn the card from step two, the card you placed facedown, the card that represents the final outcome.

6) Looking at all of the cards, knowing what you see there, ask yourself the following questions:

1. Does the card representing the final outcome mesh with my personal goals for the future?

2. Would I be willing to compromise these goals to accommodate a mate?

3. Are the attributes I'm looking for in a mate realistic, or are they idealized?

You can interpret the final card using your own intuition and the card's general meaning, or you can view this card as a yes/no answer using the yes/no guide for the cards posted with the last reading.

Money/Wealth Spreads

Money...We need a certain amount of it to exist; we need a more specific amount to live a comfortable and fulfilling life; and we need a hell of a lot more money to role in hedonistic orgasmic self-indulgence. The majority of us just want to be able to pay our bills, keep a roof over our head, food on the table, and be able to successfully chase the middle-class suburbian dream.

The following tarot spreads will help us make decisions that directly affect the flow of money to our bank accounts and, thus, to our households.

I. Should I change jobs?

1) Lay three cards representing your present job.
Look closely at these cards, very closely, and study them. This is where you're at right now. Do you see something here you

weren't expecting, or something that you don't want to admit out loud?

2) Lay three cards representing a new job.
Look at these cards closely and study them. This may be where you're going. Do you like what you see here?

3) Lay three cards representing the positive aspects of your present job.
Honestly, are there more positive aspects to your job than you realized or were willing to admit; or is it worse than you thought?

4) Lay three cards representing the positive aspects of a new job.
Do you see unexpected perks here, maybe pleasant surprises that you weren't expecting. Does this group of cards seem more appealing than the group of cards in step three?

5) Lay three cards representing the negative aspects of your present job.
Is it really as crappy as you've been telling yourself, or is it worse?

6) Lay three cards representing the negative aspects of a new job.
Uh-oh, you may be surprised at what you see here, or you'll be so anxious to get away from your old job that you might try to convince yourself it's 'not that bad'.

7) Lay one card for the final outcome.
If you're doing this reading for yourself, it may be wisest to view this card as a yes/no answer. That way, at least you'll know that you won't be fooling yourself.

2. Is now the right time to start my own business?
If it's just a simple 'yes or no' that you want from this question. Draw a card and follow the guidelines for yes/no answers. However, if you want a little more insight into the situation, do

this reading:

> *1) Lay three cards to view this question from a financial perspective.*
> *2) Lay three cards to view this question from a personal perspective.*
> *3) Lay three cards to view this question from a family perspective.*
> *4) Lay three cards to represent unexpected conditions.*

Now you'd better lay one card and go for a yes/no answer, but this time take into consideration the information that you've gathered, just be honest with yourself.

3. Is someone stealing from me?

I hate a thief. If you suspect that someone is pilfering your funds or belongings, odds are that someone is doing just that. However, before you go on a rampage, use this tarot spread to gather information:

1) Lay three cards to represent your friends.

These cards will not only display the familiar to you, that which you were expecting to see; these cards may also point out to you people you haven't yet allowed across the borders of your inner circle, but whom you should consider.

2) Lay three cards to represent your enemies.

Oh, how bittersweet these cards can be! You might be very surprised by a familiar face you see here, one that belongs to a 'friend'. Enemies often masquerade in the guise of friend, someone whom you've cultivated a closeness too, someone who has led you to believe they are as fond of you as you are of them. But these cards will reveal the truth. These cards will expose jealousy, concealed contempt, back-stabbing, meanness, and more.

3) Lay three cards to expose deceit.
This is like playing spin the bottle, but the winner doesn't get a kiss. This may be difficult, especially if you received some surprises in step two. You have to make yourself look. It might hurt, but look anyway.

4) Lay a card which will point to the thief.
This can be just a yes/no card if you wish; but it's really better to take this card to heart and let it speak to you. Don't ignore the whisper in your ear. Do you recognize the culprit?

Spreads for Common Questions:
I. Should I move?

This can be a simple yes/no answer combined with the following spread for a broader look at all your options and potential outcomes:

1) Lay three cards representing the advantages.
Some of what you see here will be predictable, as you've probably been mulling over advantages to moving since the idea occurred to you. But you might find a surprise or two, something that you hadn't thought of.

2) Lay three cards to represent the disadvantages.
Some of what you see here will be obvious. After all, moving (whether across town or across country) is disruptive and is a milestone in our life. But something else might pop up that you weren't expecting. The important thing about this reading, about all readings you're doing for yourself, is to be open to anything you might see. You have to be able to have enough grasp on your emotions and mentality to squelch any preconceived ideas or scenarios.

3) Lay one card for the final outcome.

I would strongly suggest that most people reading for themselves combine this card with a yes/no answer, just in case anyone using this spread is not experienced with reading the tarot, or lack the ability to step outside themselves for an objective view.

2. My Spirit Guide: How do I connect?

1) Lay three cards representing your spiritual path.

Even if you think you know why you believe what you believe, you might be pleasantly surprised to find that the influence and meaning of your spiritual practices runs deeper than you think and rises from areas within your being that you were not even aware of and that you may very well learn from.

2) Lay three cards representing feminine spiritual guidance.

Do you have a patron goddess? Have you ever even thought about it? If you don't and you haven't, you will now. She's there. She's been there all along, whether as a vague misty childhood memory, as an obsessive interest or passion, or as a quiet influence in your life, often popping up as an unexpected image in unusual ways and in the most unusual places.

3) Lay three cards representing masculine spiritual guidance.

Just as with the feminine influence revealed in step #2, these cards will point you towards your patron god and may even trigger suppressed memories of images, angels, beings, and spirits that you've encountered or dreamed throughout your life. As with the goddess, the god has always been there, your mind's eye just might have been closed to the possibility.

4) Lay three cards representing your animal totem.

Surprisingly, people are more often able to connect and recognize an animal spirit or guide rather than a temporal god, goddess, or angelic being. Our connections with the animal world run deep, and our association with a particular animal and their spirit begin very early in life.

5) You will lay six cards now in what I call a 'window', a revealing spread of cards that will give you insight into the matter at hand. These six cards are laid in the form of an inverted pyramid: three cards making up the top row; two cards the middle row; and one card at the bottom, to complete the pyramid. I use this pyramid window often, it is an open doorway, a gift from the tarot.

3. Who is deceiving me?

*1) Lay three cards for **each** suspected individual.*

This may be a short spread, or it might turn out to be a whopping big spread of cards. It's going to depend on just how many individuals you suspect of deception.

2) Lay three cards representing the individual who is actually deceiving you.

Does anything look familiar? Of course, the ideal would be to turn one of the court cards here. It would be like pointing a finger directly at the scoundrel. But the cards may have other ideas; the cards may want you to look deeper, beyond the surface issues, to the reasons behind this individual's actions. You may, or may not, like what you see.

3) Lay one card to represent the actual deception.

It may run deeper than you think, or it may turn out to be much ado about nothing. In the end, you'll have to decide whether life will run more smoothly if you just let it go, or if the issue is serious enough to warrant a confrontation.

4. Should I cast this spell?

1) Lay three cards telling you why you should.

2) Lay three cards telling you why you shouldn't.

3) Lay three cards to reveal long term effects of casting the spell.

4) Lay three cards to reveal long term effects of not casting the spell.

5) Lay one card...yes/no

Now the question will be:

Do you agree with the last card?

5. Will we have a safe trip?

We took lots of road trips when our kids were small, and I would usually do a reading before each trip. I would also perform a *vehicle blessing*[66] You will find a complete Vehicle Blessing in my book, **"The Gray Witch's Grimoire"**. For more information, go to, often right out in the driveway in full view of the neighbors. Safety comes first, and as far as dealing with curious questions, I would tell anyone who inquired that both of my great-grand-mothers had a healthy dose of Native American blood running through their veins. It's funny how quickly the public accepts shamanic practices of certain indigenous people, never realizing that their own European heritage is full of the same magic.

1) Lay three cards to represent any stumbling blocks to your plans.

You may or may not find anything here, and if you do, don't be surprised if it's as mundane and miniscule as scheduling glitches or minor detour issues.

2) Lay three cards for each of the cards you just laid in step #1.

Be particularly aware of cards that come up such as The Tower, ten of swords, The Chariot reversed, and the nine of cups reversed. If any of these cards come up, lay three more cards for that particular card to give you more insight.

3) Lay one last card...yes/no

6. My Dream: What does it mean?

Dreams are so enigmatic and so subjective that I have never used a dream dictionary or reference book. I've browsed through a few out of curiosity, but I quickly discovered that my associations with an object, an animal, or a situation, might mean something completely different to me than it did to the author of the reference book. I have, however, used the tarot cards to give me insight into my dreams, particularly dreams that seem to have a purpose: prophetic dreams to enlighten me or to warn me of something, past life dreams that have given me a glimpse into my own phobias and déjà vu moments, and dreams that appear to be messages from the deceased.

1) Lay a window, the six card tarot pyramid, as I described previously.
Take your time and study these cards, sit with a cup of coffee or tea perhaps, and let your mind relax and wander. You might be very surprised to discover that information which was coming to you in your dream will continue and expand while you are immersed in this reading. Sometimes I do this with a pen and notebook in hand, and I jot down particular bits of information or revelations that come to me consciously during this reading.

2) Lay three cards for any card in the tarot pyramid, if you feel you need more clarification for that particular card.

7. Where is it?: Finding Lost Objects

1) Lay one card for every possible location you have thought of. Lay these cards in a straight row.
Include in this row of cards any location that may have popped into your head, even if you don't logically think that it's correct. We're here to listen to your sub-conscious mind, not the logical side of yourself, which often thinks inside the box by habit.

2) Lay three cards representing the actual location of the missing object. Do any of these three cards share a connection with one of the cards you laid in step one? If so, this is where you'll find the missing object. This type of reading is one where the connection you might see is either whimsical, a quick and unexpected recognition between two images on a pair of cards; or it might be that little voice in your head that suddenly speaks up with a suggestion.

8. Am I in danger?

If you feel that you are in danger, and you feel it strongly enough to do a tarot reading about it, lay one card immediately for a yes-no answer.

Lay a pyramid window for more information and insight. Pay close attention to court cards and the individuals they represent, to any cards depicting confrontations, The Moon- deception, the Ten of Swords, or The Tower.

After doing this reading, confide in someone you trust, if you haven't already.

9. Will my project be successful?

1) Lay three cards representing your goals for this project.
2) Lay three cards representing any obstacles to this project.
3) Lay a pyramid window for more insight into the project and it's future as a whole.
4) Lay one card for a yes-no answer.

10. Who will help me?

1) Lay three cards for each individual you expect help from.
2) Lay three cards for three unknown individuals who may help you.
You may see someone in the last three cards that you haven't

even met yet. Pay attention to any court cards, cards relating to your work and work place, and cards relating to family and relationships.

Tarot Readings

I keep on file every written reading I do, and I retain the copyright to all readings, including the private readings that are emailed to my clients. I've gone through all of this material, and I've chosen a variety of readings to include in this book just to let you get an idea of how the tarot works for me. Every tarot experience is uniquely personal, so I can't tell you that this is how it will work for you, but have no doubt that the way in which you connect with the cards will be exceptional to your personality and how you process information.

Past Life Reading

Through the magick of the tarot and the intuitive ability of the reader, you can learn about your past life. Who were you? What period of history did you live in? How did you make your living, and how did you relate to the people around you? By learning about your past life, you add to the experience, knowledge, and fulfillment of your present life. You may discover why you're drawn to particular historical times and places; why you experience incidents of deja'vu; why you keep attracting a particular type of partner or friend.

By learning about your past life, you have the opportunity to make educated decisions in this life that will also affect future incarnations.

The tarot spread for a past life reading includes fourteen cards laid to cover the following topics:

1. Basic Soul Nature/upon entering this life

2. Environment
3. Early Years
4. Education
5. Accomplishments
6. Occupation
7. Social Status
8. Relationships
9. Family Life
10. Death
11 & 12. Lessons Learned
13 & 14. How your past life affects your present life.

Note: The following past life reading is an actual reading done for a client. Thank you to "M".

I. Basic Soul Nature
Eight/swords

You tend to limit yourself by not being very adventurous when it comes to trying new things. You are confined and defined by other people's opinions. You allow yourself to be restrained and contained by circumstances and people in your life, and you allow this mostly through apathy and laziness. You tend to follow the path of least resistance. This can mean that you withhold honest opinions, or any opinion at all, and you will never side with the underdog because that would mean more work and effort. This often sets you apart from those you would otherwise share a connection with.

You are a soul trapped by mitigating circumstances, and to relieve yourself of the inner nature that allows this, that is in order to change, you will have to find your voice and strength of will.

2. Environment
The Hermit ®

You lived in isolation, which is a circumstance that contributed to your inability to verbally express yourself with success or ease. You lived in a manner that didn't require a lot of interaction. I'm seeing a staff and feel that your life revolved around agriculture, livestock, the outdoors. You were connected to the earth and it's cycles so closely that this aspect of your past life has carried over for many lifetimes, and to this day, this is your strongest connection. Sometimes the environment in this past life was harsh; you faced the elements at their most basic. Winter seems to have left an indelible impression in this aspect, as it was the most rugged to survive.

3. Early Years
Page/pentacles ®

You were wild in the youth of your past life. You were earthy and felt no qualms about satisfying your whims and urges. For many reasons, some of them being your unorthodox behavior and your inability to make solid emotional connections to people, you were isolated, or you felt isolated, from those close to you, those within familial or community settings. However, there's one thing that you had no doubts about, and that was your connection to the earth and the lifestyle that accompanied the farmer or the peasant in a rural setting. Through the haze that has been your experience with human relationships, this is the one contact that has always been strong and clear. You knew early what it was you wanted to do and where you belonged.

4. Education
The Moon

Your education was sketchy, often based on superstition, as well as ancient wisdom and practices. This past life reaches far back into ancient times, before the dawning of the Renaissance, before the first ages of enlightenment, even before Christianity had reached the vast majority of what we now call Europe, but just on the cusp of this change. You lived by the laws and knowledge of nature, rather than the precepts and wisdom of the early scholars.

5. Accomplishments
The Magician ®

Many of your attempts to accomplish goals in this past life were thwarted by a lack of power, incentive, energy, direction, or the acceptance of those around you. What you did accomplish in this past life was connected to the elements, and the Elements, as in the occult use of Earth, Air, Fire, and Water. One problem was that you often found that your ideas, which may have been ahead of the times, were not readily received or accepted by friends, family, or community. Because of your nature, it was just easier to follow the general path and forget about those goals and dreams that only you could see as worthy and attainable. This may be an issue that plagues you all the way to your present life.

6. Occupation
4/Swords

Your occupation centered around a rural and agricultural setting. You may not have been as successful in your occupation as you could have been because you often lacked ambition, but also because you suffered from some sort of physical infirmity which often prevented you from successfully completing physical tasks. You tired easily, were sick often, and lacked a strong constitution. You were also an individual within the community whose job it was to help dispose of the dead. Your life was touched by those spirits in numerous positive, as well as negative, ways.

7. Social Status
The Chariot ®

Although you were not at the top of the social ladder, you were well within the upper echelon. In spite of any hindrances you might have faced with your occupation, both those brought on by your own nature and those beyond your control, you were well respected within your community and you made a fairly good living for the time that this was. You lived slightly above the average standards and provided well for your family. It appears that within your community, you were often called upon to help make important decisions, implying that you were counted among the leaders of this particular area or village.

8. Relationships
The Hierophant

Your stubborn personality and terrifically conformist views made relationships in this lifetime difficult, and it's possible that this type of behavior has carried over into many lifetimes. You had difficulty seeing a world outside of black and white, or defining personal boundaries of freedom for your partners. Within this past life you had more than one mate, possibly several, some lost to illness, some to wars and famine and other catastrophes of this age. You were plagued in this lifetime with a series of broken relationships, and this pattern may still continue with each incarnation. You've spent an eternity seeking your soul mate, and it is a search that has so far been unsuccessful, but a search that you refuse to abandon.

9. Family Life
Eight/cups ®

The most frustrating thing about family relationships in this past lifetime is that someone was always leaving, whether it was because of death or personal decisions. This leads you to a feeling of abandonment, or a fear of abandonment, that may persist to this day. It's also indicated that you have a tendency to abandon a relationship when it becomes difficult, when it requires more verbal interaction and emotional depth than you are prepared or able to give. It also seems that you were forever in search of something intangible, possibly seeking approval, seeking love and connection and attention, seeking some aspect of a relationship that you were never quite able to find. This search is most likely still underway.

10. Death
Seven/swords

Your death in this lifetime was brutal and violent, possibly death by the sword, as would be befitting this ancient era. The perpetrator was a thief or someone who owed you a great deal of money, land, or goods, possibly a business partner. The sad thing is that it seems he was most likely successful at the end and either kept those things which were your due, or robbed you further from your estate posthumously, carrying away many of your belongings, livestock, etc. The odd thing is that this individual may very well touch your life in the same negative way in the present lifetime, not quite as dramatically as in this past life, but more as someone that you may have connected with through business deals of a very negative nature, business deals that led to bad financial decisions and outcomes.

Lessons Learned During Your Past Life:
11. Eight/pentacles

One of the most important things you learned from this past life is to have a strong work ethic, to concentrate on developing your occupation, to apply yourself where needed to learn your craft, and to grow in the knowledge and talent needed for whatever career you have chosen in this lifetime.

12. Nine/wands

You've learned, through unfortunate events in your past life, to not be quite so trusting of everyone who comes along. You've learned to protect yourself and stand up for your opinions, beliefs, and decisions. This is all very well and good, as long as you don't become overly suspicious and paranoid about people and their motives.

How This Past Life Affects Your Current Life:
13. King/pentacles

There is an individual who you keep meeting from one lifetime to the next, and you've not yet learned how to protect yourself from this individual's negative control and influence. You will keep meeting this character until you gain enough self-respect and self-confidence to stand up to this person. You will keep confronting this individual from one lifetime to the next until you loose your fear of them.

14. Seven/pentacles ®

You've learned well the importance of working diligently to create a financial nest egg to support your future. You've learned the value of the dollar; you've learned the virtue of hard work; and you've learned to accept success with grace.

Missing Person/Criminal Case Readings

I'm very excited about the idea of using psychics and their methods to solve criminal cases, and for several years I've often felt the compulsion to do readings for cases that are making headlines. I've never been quite sure that the information I gather from this practice would give enough detailed information to be of concrete use to the authorities, and I've never contacted the authorities in any of these cases to give them the information that I've recorded from my endeavors. But, for some reason, I still feel compelled to do these readings, and I don't argue with my instinct.

Below are readings for two cases that are, at the time of this writing, unsolved.

"Baby Lisa"
Lisa Irwin
Kansas City, Missouri
Disappeared: October 3, 2011

This reading was done on the following date:
11-8-2011

Six cards were drawn, laid in pyramid fashion, i.e. three cards at the top in the first row, two cards beneath that, and a single card at the bottom. I call this my 'window', and this gives me a basic foundational look at the overall picture. To expand this information, that is to learn more from any one of the cards laid in this original spread, I will remove this card from the pyramid and draw three more cards for it. This is the general way I begin a reading.

The Pyramid:
Knight/wands ®.........10/wands ®.........Queen/pentacles
10/swords.........2/wands ®
2/swords

First impressions: *As I begin turning the cards with my left hand, I have a pen in my right hand and I begin jotting down whatever comes into my mind, whether it makes any sense or not, often I am not even looking at the paper I'm writing on, but stay focused on the cards. The result is that when I refer to this sheet of paper, I will see things written all over it in a helter-skelter fashion. The idea is not to think or dwell on ideas or impressions, but just to jot them down as quickly as they pop into my head, the reason being that I'm running with my sub-*

conscious mind.

The following narrative is my first impression of these cards:

Ran away/charging to the rescue/thundering, pounding/arrogant & loyal/a waning moon/a leather belt/a crossroads, water, butterflies/a great burden or weight/a woman who does not see, denial/blind/denial/a pile of logs or wood, feathers, reptiles/waiting by the water/reptiles, wood, feathers/the mother /earth/garden/poppies/logs, trees, timber/a stone barrier/butterflies, moths, water/death, cut, stabbed, pierced

Second impressions: *After jotting down the first impression of each individual card, I'll look at the pyramid as a whole and see what type of information, if any, unfolds. Most of the time, the cards will tell a story:*

The first thing that comes to mind is that two individuals are involved in Baby Lisa's disappearance, and these individuals share a deep connection or partnership of some kind. The ten of swords, in my readings, is the closest that comes to any card for showing a death. At any rate, it's never a good sign and generally smacks of foreboding dark energy. The female character involved in Lisa's disappearance either acted rashly, not thinking things through clearly, or she was not the major participant in this event, but rather was more of an accomplice. Her main contribution to this scenario right now is her lack of will to reveal needed information.

At this point, I'm going to draw more cards for some of the original cards first laid to expand the story:

Queen of Pentacles
7/wands ®.........The Magician.........Page/pentacles ®
The Queen, I feel, represents the female involved in Lisa's disap-

pearance, and I believe that in this case, it may be a maternal figure. This is a woman who feels caught between two strong male figures, which leaves her with a sense of helplessness in some aspect and an inability to act on her own, either because of intimidation, or the desire to protect someone.

The following cards, The Magician and the Page of pentacles, seems to represent two separate male figures, and one of them possesses more control in this situation than the other. One has more power and a dominant position within the triangle, and one is more reckless and questionable, both in character and behavior. The page indicates that one of these male figures may be considerably younger than the other.

The seven of wands indicates conflict within this group, which can include power plays, petty disagreements, and feelings of defensiveness.

10/swords
The Tower ®.........3/cups ®.........The Sun ®
These cards indicate that there was some cataclysmic event which most likely led to the injury or death of Baby Lisa. The cards point to three individuals being involved, though it's not clear whether these individuals were all involved together at the moment of the event, or whether someone came into this scenario after the fact. The cards do leave me with the impression that whatever this horrific event was, it may have been an accident at the beginning, leading to a conspiracy to hide the fact afterwards.

The reading above offers a scenario, along with a cast of possible suspects or characters connected to the story. However, the fact remains that someone is physically missing and more detailed information is required in order to find this person. Tarot cards don't provide this type of information for me. In order to gather more detailed data through psychic means, I used a map and my pendulum.

This first pendulum reading done here, is done with a rough hand-drawn map that gives me perimeters stemming from the original location, in this case the house and yard, and gradually broadening out mile by mile from the central spot. I take it one step at a time, beginning in the center of the map, which in this case is the house, and moving in an ever widening circle, asking precise questions as I go. The four cardinal points of the compass are also indicated on this map— north, east, south, and west.

1. Is Baby Lisa physically within the house?
No

2. Is Baby Lisa physically within the garage?
Yes. The pendulum indicated that evidence could be found in this area. On my hand-drawn map, I added a 'garage' onto the east side of the building, though in reality, I'm unfamiliar with the house and grounds. I just wanted to be able to exclude a garage or attached garage, if there is one; and I inadvertently added this attachment to the east side of the main location (the house).

3. Is Baby Lisa physically in the yard, or on the grounds, that goes with this house?
Yes. Apparently there is evidence that can be found in this area. I haven't been following this case closely, so I'm not sure what may already have been discovered, if anything, or where, so I want to narrow this general question down to be more specific about the direction within the yard where this evidence can be found.

4. Is Baby Lisa physically located in the north side of the yard?
No

5. Is Baby Lisa physically located in the west side of the yard?
No

6. Is Baby Lisa physically located in the south side of the yard?
No

7. Is Baby Lisa physically located in the east side of the yard?
Yes. Once again, the pendulum gave a positive response when held over the map on the east side of the main location, which is the house. I don't know if there is a garage on this side of the building, but if there is, or if there is an outbuilding of some kind located here, it's indicated that evidence can be found in this location. It might also be that evidence was already found in this location and just not revealed to the public.

Karen Swift
Location: Dyersburg, Tennessee
Disappeared: October 30, 2011
Body Found: December 10, 2011

Note: For this reading, I didn't use a traditional deck of tarot cards. I used *"The Psychic Tarot Oracle Deck"*, a sixty-five card deck by John Holland. It was the first time I ever used this deck.

This reading was done on the following date:
1-2-2012

The cards drawn:
Destiny...Transformation...Patience

I got three basic pieces of information from this reading: 1) why Karen Swift left the house, and left at such an unusual time; 2) an important item that needs to be found; 3) the initials, and eventually the names, of two individuals who are either directly involved with Karen's fate or they are privy to information about the case that they may not have shared.

1) Karen Swift left her house at the odd hour she did in such a hurry because she was afraid. Karen's husband David was jealous, and they argued. She fled in fear.

2) Among Karen's personal possessions is a notebook in which she wrote down details of confrontations with David (her husband), her personal feelings, fears, etc.

Karen kept a detailed record of arguments and outbursts.

Find this book.

3) The initials "D" and "J" came up. The "D" stands for "David"; the "J" stands for "James". Who is James? This man needs to be found. He's either directly connected to this crime, or he is privy to valuable information regarding this case.

Celebrity Readings

Can you read the tarot for strangers, someone that you don't know and have never met? Yes, you can. Is it ethical? This is debatable, depending on which side of the fence you're on when it comes to reading for someone without their explicit request or permission. I've chosen two very enigmatic and popular women to include in this section, two women who have chosen to open themselves and their lives up to the public by seeking the spotlight. I chose these women for a variety of reasons. 1) I feel that other women can learn from these women about such things as ambition, hard work, and success; 2)-I feel that these women showcase their strengths and have learned to overcome any weaknesses, and if they haven't quite conquered them all, they're working on it; 3) I chose these women because they have so much to tell and so much more depth to their characters than is publicly acknowledged; 4) I chose these women because they are exceptional.

*Disclaimer:

For legal purposes I should state that neither of the celebrities listed below have ever sought out me or my psychic services. These "Celebrity Readings" are entirely my own opinions of public personalities, the conclusions of which I arrived at through the tarot cards drawn randomly for each individual. The results of these readings are not based on facts, but on my own intuition and interpretation of the cards.

Madonna

(This reading was done on 1-15-2012)
Page/swords...5/swords...4/wands ®
8/cups ®...The Word
4/pentacles

First impression: Her life is an infusion of tough messages and petty battles. Whenever there's something to celebrate in her life, the celebration always seems to fall under the shadow of controversy, bad feelings, or personal crises. Someone is always leaving, and when they do the results are unfinished business. The four of pentacles tells me that she's wiser about handling her money affairs than I would've thought, or she's a miser, or both. At any rate, at this time there are ties and restraints of some kind in place where money is concerned.

Page/swords: It must get exhausting to be constantly battling the world and everyone in it, to feel as though everything she believes in and strives for has to be fought for to be achieved. The tension of feeling as though she is constantly on guard will wear upon this woman in a variety of ways, both emotionally and physically. (*What do you think will happen if you let your guard down?*) The feeling of vulnerability is so distasteful to this individual, that no matter how old she lives to be, she will, as long as she is able, keep a shield and sword figuratively at the ready, in order to squelch the unfortunate soul who tries to break through this armor.

5/swords: The feistiness is so dominate, and a sense of competition that goes over the top, as it often does with people who are successful. The thing is, that there will come a point in life, if she lives long enough, where she can't keep this up. You can't remain on the front lines of life's battles forever. Eventually this will become an issue that negatively affects a variety of areas in her life and all the people who live there. And so she wins this battle and that battle, and she gets what she wants. But what is the fallout from this victory? Who are the victims? What did she really win?

The tactics demonstrated by this card may well be a form of self-preservation. This woman tends to strike out first, in order to keep herself from being hurt. She doesn't want the world to see how sensitive she actually is. She may even view her sensitivity as a weakness.

4/wands ®: Life's celebrations and high points have come at a tremendous price. For every step forward, this woman has often had to take two steps backwards. There is an underlying sense of sadness. No matter how much she accomplishes, no matter what the happy personal milestones she reaches, there is a sense that it's never enough. There's never enough happiness to compensate for the sadness.

But it's not a catch up game. That's what she has to realize.

8/cups ®: This card speaks of leaving, both other people leaving

Madonna's life, and her leaving their's. There's a sense of darkness about it, in that it suggests someone turning their back. When someone turns their back on you, it isn't the same as just leaving. Turning your back on someone implies a lack of respect, a negative interpretation placed on everything in their world. It hurts more than when someone just leaves.

The World: Madonna is working on a project now which will come to fruition in the near future. If not, this card tells me that the opportunity is coming. This is the only card in this spread which gives me a sense of peace and satisfaction. In it, this woman is in her element. This card speaks of power in creativity, of satisfaction in completion. But it also speaks of isolation in some form, isolation from someone she loves, from somewhere she wants to be, isolation that is not welcome. Women tend to discover that in order to find themselves, to be complete within themselves, to accomplish what they set out to do, they do all this best when they are alone.

4/pentacles: The miser. There is some area of finances in this lady's life that is tied up at the moment, an area that she has access to, and an area that she doesn't. I feel that she is figuratively 'locking up' her income in some way so as to prevent a sharing or a pilfering of these funds by another party. This card also tends to imply that this woman is more conservative in this area of life than many would realize; but it may not appear this way to the general public, the majority of people who would never be able to comprehend what access to great wealth is like.

Lady Gaga

(This reading was done on 1-21-2012)
6/cups ®......Knight/pentacles ®......The Devil ®
The Hierophant......Nine/cups ®
The Fool

First impression: Lady Gaga is heavily influenced by her past and the stability within it; she's also influenced by the dark side of this period of her life, a side laced with insecurities and personal bogeymen. At one point, I believe that she was figuratively screaming to get out or get away. Traditionalism and a touch of the conservative run through her veins, and I believe that at times this causes an inner conflict between who she really wants to be and the public persona. She appears to have gotten her wish, but it came with a price. Her journey continues.

6/cups ®: L.G. is strongly influenced by her past. The chalices on this tarot card go far beyond the usual associations. They represent the womb and are tied strongly to religion, spirituality, the feminine, and a kind of ritual figurative 'blood-letting'. Someone very close to her may not really 'get it', not deep down and truly. There's someone in her past, or an issue from her past, that needs acknowledgment and closure. She won't really be able to move on until this is done.

Knight/pentacles ®: This knight is a knight of stability, representing all that is grounded, representing approval, representing what's safe. And this knight is reversed; he's slightly 'off', maybe a little wobbly, indicating that some lines may be blurred along these matters. L.G. may sometimes find it difficult to keep a grasp on her world, feeling that things are out of control, or that she's lost a hold somewhere along the line. It's important that she stop, regroup, and gather these loose strands. If she doesn't, it could lead to greater instability in some area of her life.

The Devil ®: This card represents all those things we tie ourselves to in life which can bring us down, all our personal obsessions, addictions, and paranoia. Since this card is reversed, it tells me that L.G. is working on overcoming these things. She's fighting it. Also, I have a strong impression of a serpent. This creature, far from popular belief, does not herald anything evil or bad; on the contrary, it is a symbol for wisdom, the feminine divine, physical rejuvenation, and healing.

The Hierophant: This card screams "conventionality", and in this case, it appears to represent someone fighting conventionality to the point of an extreme. This card seems to be a warning. Sometimes this in-your-face attitude of "I'm different, I wanna' be different, I want people to see me as different" can blow up. It can backfire with unforeseen results. Extremes in general are rarely healthy. Also, a balancing of the chakras may be in order. This lady has rampant energies running all over the place. She needs to keep all this energy aligned and working properly.

9/cups ®: "The Wish Card". She's got what she wants, but is it enough? It almost never is. (*What have you sacrificed along the way?*) I'm also getting from this card the feeling that either 1) she's surrounded herself with an inner circle of individuals who may suddenly find themselves unexpected gatekeepers in a unique position. These people may come to realize they have quite a measure of influence with their charge, and this is a questionable thing; or 2) she needs to surround herself with a solid inner circle which she might be lacking. Should L.G. read this, she'll know which it is.

The Fool: Lady Gaga's journey continues. This card simply warns her to have-a game plan, to watch where it is that she's going, and to judge wisely which is the best way to get there. Her unique dogged sense of determined concentration is highlighted within this card and the fact that someone who has passed is very near her most of the time. I'm betting that she's sensitive enough to be aware of this energy, whether she knows who it is, or not.

A Mini Reading

The following reading was done by laying three sets of triplicates (9 cards) with the tarot deck, "Golden Tarot of Klimt". You don't have to lay a whopping amount of cards to get an incredible amount of information or a great deal of perspective on a client and their situation. The Klimt deck is one of the most visually haunting that I've come across. It just has a really out-in-left-field feeling to it, and I've noticed that it tends to give me the most unusual and unexpected insights.

It is advantageous to the tarot reader to experiment with different decks, which all carry different energies. I know some readers who prefer specific decks for different types of readings and situations. I carry with me no less than three decks when doing public readings. When one deck just doesn't feel right with a client, I can switch off to another one with energy more attuned to that individual and their situation.

You can find "Golden Tarot of Klimt" at Amazon.

Death...Knave/Chalices...7/pentacles

He (the Knave) looks on without emotions as her feelings play themselves out. Behind him, hidden, are all the treasures he longed to give her. Behind him lay the one that death took, yet he faces her. Before him, at his back, stands the strong one.

10/pentacles...7/pentacles...Knight/Wands

She runs the gauntlet to keep what she has or to gain what she longs for. She thinks she's happy, but this is only an isolated moment, a surreal conclusion. Behind her is the man who will shake her from this illusion, either jarring her from her fantasy, or catapulting her into insanity.

9/swords...10/cups...The Emperor

Unity has come with a price. On one side the anguish of doubt and emotional stress; upon the other side strong arm tactics of a man. And between them both lay the crumpled pile of wounded personalities and cliques that use to masquerade as a family.

This Reading is for You

Once in a while, I'll wake up with the desire to do an anonymous reading. I don't know why; I don't know for whom; and I don't care. I just do it. The reading below is one of these anonymous readings. If this reading is for you, you'll recognize it. And, believe it or not, when I do these readings they have never failed to strike a chord with at least one individual and often with several.

The reading that I'm doing this morning is for you. I don't know who you are, how the circumstances in your life stands, or whether you will even find this reading. But I woke up this morning with the distinct feeling that someone needs this. I'm going to draw three cards for you, and these cards will be a window into your life, the people who inhabit it, and those issues that are important to you. You will recognize yourself, you will recognize the people who may show up within this group of cards; and you will know, with absolute certainty, that these cards are speaking especially to you, specifically to you, for you and you alone.

The cards:
Ace/cups......3/wands......2/pentacles

You're just beginning a new relationship, perhaps you're even in transition yet, moving from one relationship to the next. This process can be fraught with indecision, that type of second guessing that makes your movement through life feel jerky. There are times that you may even carry around a rock in the pit of your stomach. So many of life's big changes are like that, and relationships are one of the biggest. But you will get through it. That heavy stone-like feeling in your mid-section will go away, and what seemed new and slightly scary will become routine so quickly that you almost won't notice the transition.

In order to successfully make this transition, and in order to work towards this new relationship with hopes that it will grow into something lasting and important, you will have to work through issues of defensiveness and insecurity– the scum that's usually left over from previous experiences. This will take time and patience, both on your part, and on the part of your new partner, or your potential partner. This can also be a measuring stick for the character of this new person in your life. They should be sensitive enough to your feelings that they respect your wishes, whatever those boundaries may be at this time.

Eventually life will come full circle, it always does, right up until the end. This is one of those things we can be sure of, just like death and taxes, as the old saying goes. The most important thing to remember is not to hinder your own freedom with your own hang-ups. It's bad enough when other people impact our lives with restrictions and invisible boundaries we don't want and didn't ask for; but it's even worse when we do this to ourselves. How many things in life we might never accomplish or leave unfinished, because we didn't allow ourselves to proceed naturally. Proceed naturally now. What else can you do?

The number three is relevant to you and your life at this moment; and I feel that this has to do with the area of relationships. It's very possible that you can't move forward because you are still staked to one spot, to one person, or point of contact. If you don't learn to let go, to move on, to forgive, to give up and get on with it, to slide on by to the next level, you will stagnate. Life is a series of progressions. Life is constant movement, sometimes so swift and relentless that it makes us dizzy. But life is never suppose to be still, at least not the type of still that prohibits new growth. Lift one foot and take that first step. The second step will be easier. I promise. It always is.

Though you may keenly feel life's burdens at this moment, that will change. You're at the threshold of a new day, a new dawn. Once you take that first hesitant step towards your future, the rusty cogs and wheels of life will begin turning again. They might be a little stiff and noisy at first, but the more they move, the smoother the journey will become. Sometimes it's just getting started that's the hard part.

You're struggling with finding balance now, but your struggle is one that will smooth out naturally, all on it's own. Don't fight it so much. When you do this you are actually working against your own energy. This will make you tired. The last thing I'm going to tell you, and maybe the most important, is not to take off on life's grand adventure without a game plan, your game plan. When you start a journey, you should have a destination in mind, otherwise how will you know when you've arrived?

Ghost Reading[77]

I have long suspected that information I was getting from readings done for criminal cases was coming from the spirits of victims who were deceased.

Connecting with the Spirit World through Tarot

I decided, one snowy afternoon in February, to try something new with my tarot cards. I set myself up with The Goddess tarot deck and a Ouija board as my table and invited a spirit who had passed over to come forward and communicate with me through the cards. The idea of doing this had come to me after I used a pendulum earlier in the day to ask if there was a spirit in the room with me. The pendulum had said 'yes'; and I wanted to know more.

Prince/swords 7/cups ® Oppression

The first card, the Prince, gives the impression of sharp objects, perhaps someone who worked with knives or some other sharp cutting tools, or machinery of this nature; a difficult life, a string of bad luck; a series of unfortunate events, messages, or relationships. Also, something that is held close to the heart. Whatever this might be, this individual, even in death, feels affection or love for someone or something that is intense. Whatever this bond was in life, it is so strong that death can't break it.

Decisions to make, several of them, leading to a period of confusion, possible mental overload, or an individual suffering from mental issues. This person may have been in an unconscious state, a coma, or a state of mental dementia for some time before they passed.

Death for this individual came as a welcome release from mental anguish. At death, this individual experienced the sensation of 'awakening' upon passing over, finding themselves in a totally unfamiliar place on the other side. Although initially confusing, I don't feel it was a negative experience.

I'm also picking up a 'mirror image', a double, perhaps a twin. The energy of this spirit feels male, and I don't believe that this person was into their elderly years when they passed. I feel that they were probably middle-aged when they crossed over.

By the time I got to the end of this reading, a mental image of this spirit had formed in my mind with more detail than I had expected:

I believe that, when this individual passed, it was a middle-aged male; divorced at least once, but more likely two or more times. The mental issues he had probably contributed to his inability to maintain a stable relationship. His work-life centered around manufacturing and machinery of some type that had blades & was used for cutting. He was either a twin, or he had a sibling that was very close to his age, and they were very tight, at least at some stage of their lives. He may have been ill for quite some time before he passed away, because the dream-like unconscious state came through very strongly. In the physical realm he was of medium build, heavy and stocky but not overweight, balding, ruddy complexion.

Triplicates:[88]
You'll find more information on 'triplicates' in the section of this book titled, *"Your Tarot Journal"*.

The Power of Three
I will often choose a quiet morning to sit down at the kitchen table in my cozy little corner, with that special first cup of morning coffee, and do several super-mini tarot readings using a simple three card spread otherwise known as 'Triplicates'. Below is one of these mini-reading sessions, mostly done for family and friends, and they will find their initials at the beginning of the reading which pertains to them. But some of these readings come up anonymously, the cards revealing information that someone out there must need. Are you here? Is one of these readings meant for you? Do you see your situation in any of these spreads?

Note: These readings were done on:
Sunday, August 21, 2011
(Deck: Rider/Waite)

1. 3/wands, Temperance, 2/wands:
Someone is apparently having quite a time keeping a balance in their lives where partnerships are concerned. I feel that business/financial partnerships are highlighted, but that is not the only kind of partnership portrayed here. Get a grip, a handle, on all these connections. Sort them out, nix the ones that are not beneficial to you, and nurture the ones that you wish to keep.

2. 3/cups, Page/pentacles, 9/swords:
A., you seem to be stressing over an occasion or get-together, possibly a celebration of some kind. Where is all the stress coming from? This appears to be a happy occasion, but that's not going to be what it feels like if you don't straighten out the issues that are making it stressful.

3. The Moon, 4/cups, The Chariot:
Oh, boy. Someone is lying to themselves about an issue that they'd rather not acknowledge or deal with, and this is going to get them no where fast. The truth might be unpleasant to face, but isn't living with a false impression almost worse? Buck up and get it over with. Life will feel better afterwards, really.

4. Ace/cups, King/wands, Knight/swords:
D., you're still living in the past, hanging onto the memories of a relationship that no longer exists. The future isn't going to be much brighter when you run into this sword. Brace yourself for bad news, really bad news; but as bad it is, it may not come as a surprise. I think you might be expecting it. Best piece of advice to you…stop nurturing your delusions.

5. Judgment, Page/wands, The Lovers:
B., you tend to judge others so harshly that it interferes with the normal flow of relationships in your life. My advice to you–lighten up. No one is perfect, including yourself, but until you realize this, you will inadvertently keep sabotaging your connections to people in your life.

6. 10/cups, 4/swords, Wheel of Fortune:
A happy family is wonderful, until it becomes suffocating. Everyone needs a time-out once in a while, no matter how much they love each other, or how close they feel they are. The individual needs room to breathe and grow, to create and cultivate...new ideas, plans, goals, decisions. Something is coming full circle, be prepared for changes afoot.

7. 10/pentacles, Knight/wands, Queen/swords:
J., there's a woman involved in your life in some way who's in a position of authority, and this woman has control of money/financial issues. If this is work related, and I feel it may be, your best bet would be not to tick her off. There's a pecking order in this situation, and you'd do well to learn your place in it.

8. The Devil, The Hermit, The Hanged Man:
Wow, this is a major pity party fed by your own demons and your dogged stubborn nature. It's time to stop feeling sorry for yourself, get a grip on those things that have dominion over you, and grow a spine. Yes, people might feel sorry for you at the moment, but how long do you think you can feed on this?

9. Ace/swords, 8/pentacles, 9/wands:
Someone on the job is feeling a little defensive lately. You might have reason too, you might not; but either way, allowing others to see your true feelings is not going to help your cause in this situation. Best thing to do is keep your head down, don't confide

in anyone– that's ANYONE– at work, and keep doing your job to the best of your ability.

10. Ace/pentacles, King/pentacles, Strength:
Someone from the grave is still trying to run the show, probably through surviving family members, legalities, and pure stubbornness that persists even in the spirit world. Grit your teeth and stand your ground. The heirs don't have his finesse, they won't be able to pull off half the shit this King used to get away with when he was alive.

11. 9/cups, 8/wands, 3/pentacles:
You're waiting for news about a job. It's coming, and it's coming very soon. Relax, you'll get what you wish for...thing is, be careful what you wish for.

12. High Priestess, Ace/wands, The Sun:
Someone is beginning a new venture, possibly business related. Listen to your gut instincts on this, including impressions of people you may be hooking up with for this venture. Whether it turns out to be a happy ending or not will depend upon how much you trust yourself and your own ability to make decisions.

13. 6/pentacles, Queen/pentacles, Justice:
M., no, your money situation right now isn't fair and there is no justice in it. But, big 'but' here, how much of this did you bring on yourself with poor decisions and an inability to curb your tendency to spend? I hate to say this, but I know you, and you've kind of dug your own grave when it comes to this predicament. Now you're going to have to work to dig your way out.

14. 5/pentacles, 2/swords, Page/pentacles:
T., you may have bit off more than you could chew financially and now it's coming back to bite you in the ass. You're faced with a lot of decisions because of this, and you're going to have to sit

down and come up with a game plan to keep your head above water and stay one step ahead of creditors. Times are tight. Don't beat yourself up. You couldn't have seen this coming.

15. 5/wands, 7/pentacles, The Magician:
There's a bickering squabbling group out there all wrapped up in a disagreement over money, might be quite a nice little wad of money, too. Who's going to come out ahead?...the individual who's not afraid to wield a little power.

16. The Star, 10/wands, 7/cups:
Yes, life is tough right now, but it doesn't have to be. Whenever you learn to break bad patterns, both from this life and past-lives, and start making better decisions, you'll find light at the end of the tunnel– surprise, surprise.

17. 4/pentacles, The World, 5/cups:
Your stubborn miserly attitude is going to come full circle, and you'll regret it. The thing you find most important, that you're working so hard to hang onto, is the very thing you're going to drive away if you don't straighten up and loosen up, both with your money and your emotions.

18. 9/pentacles, 6/wands, 7/swords:
There's a lady who feels she's won it all, her heart's desire. Truth is, she hasn't won anything. The people around her are leading her on, stealing her blind, taking advantage of her in numerous ways, both financially and emotionally. Don't be so easily played. Are you really so naïve that you have to believe everything everyone tells you? Time to grow up and take off the rose colored glasses– fast!– before you lose everything, including your dignity.

19. Knight/cups, The Empress, 3/swords:
If you're thinking about having an affair, think again. The

swords that pierce the heart on this card can just as easily strike you. If you have this affair, you are most likely going to produce a child. Are you ready for this responsibility? Are you ready to face family members with the results of your poor choices?

20. 5/swords, 9/cups, 4/wands:
Nope, you're not going to pull off this plan, and you might as well pack up the balloons and cancel the caterer. Something is amiss here, and it has to be straightened out before the decision is made to go forward as planned or take a different path. Instead of a celebration on the horizon, there will be a period of deep thinking and introspection. That's okay, this is where answers are found.

Your Tarot Journal

I encourage anyone wishing to learn the tarot to keep a journal. Take notes, keep track of information, write down your thoughts on the subject, any questions you may have, your own interpretations, resources you might run across, as well as readings and a daily card. These are all ways to build in knowledge and grow with experience. Your journal will prove to be an invaluable source for study as you add more information and self-revelations to it. And to anyone reading this who may be a seasoned reader, I still suggest keeping a journal if you don't already. The tarot journey is a never-ending composite of new experiences and revelations that adds to the magic of the cards on a daily basis.

The Cards: Your Interpretation

Create one section of your tarot journal to write down your very own very personal interpretations for each card. If your interpretation has nothing to do with the traditional meaning, so be it. You see what you see, you feel what you feel. Trust your instincts. You might want to leave two or three pages available for each card, as you will discover along the way that new interpretations will come to you the longer you use the cards.

Your Significator

Who are you? Which of the court cards do you feel an affinity with? Peel away misconceptions and vanity to take a hard look at yourself and at the personality types associated with the court cards. Who are you— really?

In the section of this book identifying the court cards, my intention was to concentrate on the dark side, because it's this side that we so often need more insight into and it's this side that causes all the problems; but for the purpose of choosing a significator, we also have to recognize the positive aspects of our own personality, and I'm going to give you a brief description here of the lighter side, the softer edge, to the court cards:

The Kings

Pentacles: This King is good with money. You might say he has the Midas touch. He also takes care of his own, taking responsibility of his brood very seriously and pushing it to new levels, and this follows his penchant for being in control. He's honest, hardworking, and loyal to a fault. If your prince charming is this King, you will never have to worry about him straying. He takes "till death do us part" quite literally.

Swords: This is the most intelligent and intellectual of the Kings. He absorbs knowledge like a sponge and can often be found in jobs where he uses his brain over brawn, very often in the professional arenas of law or finance. He has an acute knack for analysis and the patience to research for answers to difficult questions or situations. Though outwardly he may appear emotionally distant, this King feels much more deeply than you might realize and can be easily hurt.

Wands: The King of Wands has a moral compass that is beyond reproach. This character is the most spiritual of the Kings, and

95

it's his spirituality that leads him through life, influencing all of his decisions in life's most important moments. This is also a King that takes responsibility very seriously, and he usually makes for an excellent employee, parent, and life partner. His surroundings are generally as well-ordered as is his life.

Cups: This is the least verbal of the Kings, the most sensitive, and the King most attuned to his life-partner. He may not say much, but don't believe for a minute that he's not taking everything in. He has an opinion, but he's almost always very hesitant to voice it. This is the most intuitive of the Kings, and he may well know what his mate needs/wants before they ask for it. He has an old fashioned sense of chivalry; but he is a lover, not a fighter. It takes a great deal to rile this King's naturally calm nature.

The Queens

Pentacles: This Queen is the most maternal of the queens, and this strong maternal bent doesn't just manifest itself with human infants and children; it also encompasses the animal world. The Queen of Pentacles is often surrounded by animals and is deeply devoted to their care and well-being. She's very earthy and enjoys the outdoors. This Queen is not afraid to get her hands dirty in the garden, and she just might enjoy a hike through the wilds. She's also very generous and loves to bestow gifts upon those within her circle of friends and family.

Swords: Just like her counterpart, the King of Swords, this is the most intelligent and intellectual of the Queens. She's often very quiet, though she is excellent with words and can be very eloquent. You very well may find her in positions that make use of these gifts, such as law or journalism. You don't want to provoke an argument with this Queen, because if she finds herself under personal attack, her tendency is to withdraw. Because of her usually introverted nature, this Queen is quite often a single woman, or a woman who doesn't marry or find a life partner until later in life.

Wands: For the Queen of Wands the hearth and home is the heart of her world. She tends enthusiastically to her family and home life, and keeping this aspect of her world running smoothly is a top priority in her life. Her penchant for organization is not lost on this aspect of her world. She has a tendency to make lists, to keep things like birthdays written down and checked off when acknowledged. This Queen's world is ordered, everyone and everything have their place in it. You'll find this lady involved in work which requires the ability to organize, delegate, and manage.

Cups: This Queen is dreamy, usually psychic, often empathic, and she seems to exist on a level that runs at a different vibration than the rest of the world. She's creative and intelligent, though she is often pulled more to the arts rather than intellectual pursuits. In general she's sensitive, often quiet, sometimes shy, and easily influenced by her surroundings and atmosphere. The Queen of Cups is also a hopeless romantic and often pursues this enigmatic happy-ever-after ending in her relationships.

The Knights

Pentacles: This Knight is calm, quiet, sometimes shy, and always dependable. There will be no surprises here. Because of a quiet slightly introverted personality, it sometimes takes a while for this character to make friends, but once you get to know him, you will recognize a diamond in the rough. This is the most mature of the knights, and he takes responsibility very seriously very early in life. He aims to please, and you won't be disappointed.

Swords: This is the most energetic and enthusiastic of the knights.

He tends to be very intelligent, eager to absorb new information, naturally curious, and easily touched by circumstances and people around him. When he loves you, you'll know it, because it will be like an enthusiastic spaniel welcoming you home. This Knight is one whom you might find fighting for causes, upholding justice, and trying to save the world.

Wands: This young Knight absorbs information like a sponge and is usually above average intelligence. He prefers to have his personal space very orderly and clean, and this is the way he usually conducts relationships. This Knight is often so absorbed in books, reading, writing, studying, and the fine facts of mathematics or science, that he forgoes personal relationships until later in life. He abhors chaos of any kind, including loud music, gatherings where there is a large number of people, or arguments.

Cups: The Knight of Cups is a hopeless romantic and generally spends a great deal of time and effort in pursuit of the perfect mate, the perfect match. This individual is also drawn to the arts, to beautiful things, to creative endeavors, and to the finer things in life. This Knight often has a heightened awareness to the spirit world, and is very open to new-age concepts and study of the paranormal. He also usually excels at something and generally enjoys the attention his accomplishments bring him.

The Pages

Pentacles: This young adult is usually a serious student, if not actually enrolled in an institution of higher learning, they will be a student of life, seeking knowledge on their own. They tend to be quiet, usually very attractive, and they are extraordinarily sensitive to rebuffs. They also have impeccable manners and tend to treat others the way they like to be treated. This Page is very loyal to their loved ones and will stand their ground to protect family and friends.

Swords: Like all the personalities of this suit, this Page is the most intelligent and usually has a very high IQ. They tend to have a sort of tunnel vision when they are engrossed in the study of something in particular or are involved in a hobby. This Page shares all the swords outwardly cool mannerisms, which so often masks a sensitivity they try to hide. This individual will often latch onto relationships with pets in order to protect themselves from the possibility of being hurt in human relationships. It's a survival mechanism.

Wands: The most prominent aspect of this Page's personality is their work ethic. This Page is an extraordinarily hard worker. They are also fiercely loyal to friends, family, and employers. This Page can't hide his enthusiasm, no matter what the object of this enthusiasm may be. They wear their emotions on their sleeve and are highly sensitive, easily insulted. Very intelligent, when they have a desire to learn about something, they will absorb information effortlessly. Learning comes very easily to the Page of Wands.

Cups: This Page is usually very talented in some aspect of the arts, free-spirited, generous, kind, and loving. They have a keen sense of responsibility; a unique sensitivity to other people's feelings; and a talent for handling difficult people or circumstances with amazing finesse. The Page of Cups shows the most positive aspects of love through a deep feeling of responsibility towards family and friends. They tend to be very sensitive to energies around them, and they are empathic to the point of being drained by other people's emotions.

Court Cards: Family, Friends, & Acquaintances

One section of your tarot journal should be all about the court cards, and now that you've had the scoop on both the positive and negative aspects of these characters, it's time to put a face to them, a face that you can recognize.

Make a list of these cards, each one of them, and leave a few lines for each card. Go back to the top of this list and begin with the kings, the King of Pentacles...who is he? Not metaphorically speaking, but really, who is he? Your father? Uncle? Boss? Brother? As soon as you recognize this personality as an actual person, write down this individual's name behind the King of Pentacles.

You'll do the same thing with all the court cards. And don't worry if you can't do this right now, all at once. Maybe there's a personality here that you haven't met yet, but you will, and when you do you will recognize them. Match them with a court card and jot down their name. Not only does this give you a fascinating look at the psychology of the archetype behind the court card, it will make reading for yourself and your family much easier. When a court card pops up, you'll know exactly who it is.

Triplicates: Making Assessments

I read for myself on a regular basis, always with a notebook and pen in hand. When I read for myself, I prefer to use *triplicates*. This is the practice of laying three cards at a time, gleaning what you can from them, and then laying three more, continuing this process until you feel that you're not getting any more information and that you are finished. And believe me, you really will be able to know when you're done. The energy changes and feels disjointed, disconnected, and the messages become garbled, suddenly making no sense.

When I read for myself, I like to be comfortable and I like to set the mood. I light a candle and sometimes some incense. I make myself a pot of coffee or nice big mug of my favorite tea, put on some relaxation music (no vocals), and situate myself in my favorite corner with my chosen tarot deck, my tarot journal, and a pen. As I turn each set of triplicates, I take my time and jot down my first impressions, then deeper meanings, sudden revelations, and innuendoes that come to me. If I recognize someone in this set of cards, I jot down their name.

When I feel that I've gotten everything that I can from this group of cards, I lay another set. I will continue this until I feel that the cards have given me all the information they are going to give up for this session. When this happens, it's time to put the cards away for another day.

Card a Day

Many people who use the tarot for themselves (for meditation, reflection, personal insight, and growth) will pull a card a day. You might wind up using a large section of your tarot journal for this practice. If you do, it's nice to include the date; the card; a first impression; an affirmation; any premonitions; and anything else that you feel is pertinent to you and your connection with this card.

Tarot Mysteries: When Animals Speak

I read tarot using the intuitive method. This method utilizes the reader's natural psychic abilities and allows the cards to simply give a gentle nudge in the right direction for all kinds of information using symbols and images. These images often include animals.

The results have been startling in clarity and synchronicity. During one reading, there was the image of a golden tabby cat hidden in the grass, peering at me with inquisitive imploring eyes. This cat turned out to be a beloved pet belonging to my client, and this cat had passed away only months before she appeared to me in this reading upon this card. During a session with another lady, there was the image of a small white rabbit. "Who's expecting a baby?" I asked. The client squealed in delight and clapped her hand over her mouth. "We're expecting our first grandbaby in three months," she says, giggling in delight.

When animals speak, I've learned to listen. What comes through is amazing, and this fact was brought home to me most pointedly when one of my clients, who had received an emailed reading, wrote back giving me invaluable feedback and an amazing story.

Below is a portion of the reading that I sent to her regarding an animal, the owl.-Following is her response, published with her permission, unedited, just as I received it:

Amythyst:
"Again, unusual impressions coming through. If your animal totem is not the owl, it may very well be now. This animal represents wisdom and quiet fortitude, as well as strength– it is tenacious, courageous, and deadly to its prey. Sometimes animals come through to me in my readings, and it is this creature which is making it's presence felt now. If you are not adverse to a little pagan energy (and I'm pretty sure you're not), it would be beneficial for you to set up a little table with some images of the owl.

The owl is also connected to heightened perception (listen to your own intuition, follow your instincts); female magick (if you're a practitioner of the occult, now's the time to do your thing regarding these issues); and messages to and from the dead (pay attention to dreams or synchronicity that you may experience around you, someone may be trying to tell you something)…"

My Client's Response:
This gave me chills.........one of my totems is indeed the owl. There is a short story here: I have always loved owls and I don't know if you are old enough to remember the old shadow box clocks and pictures from the 70's....but my ex husband bought one with an owl on it. I ended up keeping that after we divorced. I remarried eventually and still kept this clock. I had it in our bedroom upstairs. We lived in a very old country farmhouse near Buffalo [New York]. The house needed new screens on the upstairs windows. I had the window open one summer day and had just brought up a load of laundry I folded to put away. Lo and behold on top of the closet door sat an owl, a real live owl. But at the time I wasn't a practicing witch but I knew there was something deep in me. It all came home for me 13 yrs ago and I have been a Solitary ever since. Fast forward to years later: I began calling owls at night and they would answer. I then began collecting owl figures. I was even gifted with an owl wing by a kindred friend. At the same time my mother was also collecting owls before she died. After she died last year my husband was fishing and he called me way up in NY to tell me that an owl landed on his fishing pole and stared at him for a minute and flew on. When my brother and I packed up mom's things I took her owl collection and still have it. So when you mentioned owls I instantly thought...."Whoa......there is no way you would ever know that!" That's when I realized that owl has a strong message for me and I need to listen.

Taking Matters to Heart

One of the things I find most unnerving about reading for strangers is people's often unexpected reactions to what they hear. I was informed once that a lady I did a reading for was offended by something I had said. To tell you the truth, I remember the gist of the reading, but not absolutely everything that I said while interpreting the cards. It was a very poignant reading because it involved the end of a relationship, always a difficult topic under any circumstances. It was also this lady's first tarot experience, so she was nervous, and she didn't know what to expect.

Let me explain how this process works for those who don't know. For me, as I turn the cards and view the images, thoughts, perceptions, and pictures begin flooding my mind. You will get the best reading from me if I just open my mouth and start talking as I turn the cards and before the thought or image vanishes. This means that I can't stop to weigh and measure every word that comes from my mouth during every minute of the reading. If I were to do this, the process would not work, the rhythm would be lost.

I can't pause and break my chain of thought to ask myself, "Would this person be offended if I say this or that?" If I were to do this, it would break my concentration and my psychic link to the cards. That's not to say that there are not automatic mental brakes in place should shattering thoroughly disturbing news come racing through; but honest to god, I can't weigh each word, each sentence, each concept that unfolds before me as it's happening without speaking up.

That's just the way it is, and that's just the way it works. Will you be offended by anything said in a reading? Odds are, no. But I won't guarantee that this won't happen. A psychic reading is often a very intimate experience; it allows the reader a peek at your soul– all bare and pink and fresh, with every pimple and imperfection laid out in plain site. Just remember that your reader is on your side; your reader is not there to pass judgment. And just like a doctor in a war zone, most psychics can say, "We've seen it all."

The Client Connection

I receive a lot of email from a lot of people. Some of it is predictable and mundane, some of it is feedback from my clients, and some of it is completely unexpected and totally out in left field. And let's get one thing straight here before I continue...It's okay to be out in left field. Everyone has to be somewhere.

The most troublesome messages for me come from people who admit to being under psychiatric care and on medications. Red flags go up, not because I feel anything negative or threatening from these individuals, but because I'm immediately aware of the fact that I may be dealing with a very fragile human being. This means that I should be very careful of what I say, very careful of the types of choices and actions that I present to them, and very cautious about any statements that could lead them to stop the mundane medical/psychological care they are receiving. However, this does not mean that I should not be truthful with them, while at the same time giving them as positive a reading as I can, and leaving them with something to go forward with and to build on.

The most unusual messages and requests I receive are from transsexuals, almost always men, all of them wanting to know if there is some magic spell to make them a woman, or to give them the power to go back and forth between being male or female. First, no, I tell them that I've never heard of this type of spell; and if there was one, it would most likely involve some sort of shamanic shape-shifting, rather than any solid permanent in-the-real-world physical change. I also encourage these individuals to seek counseling, to get in touch with clinics that specialize in surgery for transsexuals, and to spend time examining their inner feelings and motives about this issue.

The most difficult messages and clients to deal with are people having mundane problems in their life, usually involving love or money, and they expect that a reading from me will solve these problems. I try to emphasize that I can give them an idea, and usually an amazingly accurate idea, of what the future will hold, what the road blocks will include, and which routes will be to their advantage. In almost all of these types of readings, any self-imposed stumbling blocks are usually exposed as well, and it's very difficult to know when to reveal this information and just how much to emphasize it. It can be a very sensitive area for some people.

A woman hopelessly in love with the wrong man would rather have all her teeth pulled with no anesthetic than to be told that her true love is a scum bag and if she doesn't ditch him and heal from the negative contact and abuse she's suffered through his hands, she will continue to decline both physically and emotionally, and happiness will be something that everyone else gets to experience, but not her. Sometimes a reader can point out the obvious, but someone blinded by the strength of their emotions may not be willing to look at it. These people usually have to learn the hard way, and many of them have drug me along as their psychic, giving me a front row seat to this process. People caught up in financial difficulties can be heart wrenchingly desperate. And unless you have experienced this predicament in life, you will not understand the depth and gravity of it. Johnny Carson was speaking on his show one time about wealth. He said, "The only thing that being rich does is to alleviate the worry about not having enough money." Of course, what he was trying to emphasize is that all of the other usual human problems are still there. However, my thought was that he had been wealthy so long he had forgotten what a horrible burden it is to worry about money. All other human problems pale in comparison if you can't pay your rent or cover the basic necessities.

In situations like this, as with any other, the ups and downs, the possibilities and the pitfalls, will come through a reading. What will not come through a reading is a magical and instant fix to your financial situation. The tarot cards give us a picture of what was, what is, and what may be coming for the future, but we will still have to stumble along and live through this human condition one day at a time, and sometimes it's a damn long rough road.

I've met some incredible people through my work, often people who have no idea how frustrating, or how inspiring, they are. As I continue to use my gift to enlighten and to enrich lives; I whole-heartedly accept the gift of enlightenment and enrichment I receive back.

Tarot Magick

I often use the tarot in my magickal practices. I have decks that are used specifically for this purpose. Some of these decks are used in ways that preserve the card so that it can be used another day for other magick, such as placing a card on my altar to help focus energy. And then there are decks I keep which will be expendable. The cards will be used in such a way as to destroy it, either by burning it in the flame of a spell candle, burying it in the earth with the remnants of a spell, or some such way, you get the idea. You may want to purchase a deck that you keep just for magickal purposes, or buy some used decks that you can pick up cheap.

Following are spells I've created specifically for this book and for use with my "Queen's Oils". These oils are aligned to the four elements, as are the Queens themselves. If you don't have Queen's Oils, you can substitute another oil for your spell, one that's aligned to the element of the Queen who's energy, and card, you're using.

The Queens' Oils

The four court cards for the Queens, found in traditional tarot decks, carries the energy of the four elements:

Earth– Queen of Pentacles
Air– Queen of Swords
Fire– Queen of Wands
Water– Queen of Cups

I've developed four magickal oils that carry the essence of each of these Queens, and I'm posting spells here to use in conjunction with 1) the tarot card connected to each Queen; 2) the oil created for each Queen[99] If you don't have any of the Queens' Oils on hand, you can substitute an oil of your choice. For more information on The Queen's Oils:
[; 3) corresponding herbs and stones; 4) candles in colors corresponding to each Queen and her element:

Queen of Pentacles- green (Earth)
Queen of Swords- yellow (Air)
Queen of Wands- red (Fire)
Queen of Cups- blue (Water)

Queen of Pentacles Magick

Magick for the Queen of Pentacles will be heavy and grounded in matters of material issues such as money, prosperity, and opportunity. The magical energy from this Queen will also encompass issues of the physical body, its health and well-being. Her connection is to the element of Earth, and this is where her energy is deeply rooted.

Spell:
To Manifest Your Desire

We're talking about a physical manifestation of something that you want, whether it be money, a new house, a better car, or some other physical item you long to have. We're also talking about manifestation of something you want, but something that is not made of molecules and atoms, whether it be a new job, success with an endeavor, a dream vacation, or something else that is very real, yet not an actual physical object.

Correspondences for Manifestation Spell

Day: Thursday
Planet: Jupiter
Moon Phase: waxing to full
Colors: Earth/green; Jupiter/purple
Oil: Queen of Pentacles Oil
Herbs: Earth/patchouli (included in the oil);
Jupiter/cloves, sage, star anise
Stones: malachite, mystic topaz, peridot
Incense: patchouli

Other items:

1. an image of your desire,
or a written explanation of your desire
2. a green candle
3. a fireproof container

The Method

Gather all the necessary items together for this spell, including an image of what you're going to manifest, or a piece of paper upon which you've described *exactly* what it is you're going to manifest. It's recommended that magick be cast within a sacred space, but this is not a written rule. If you're not comfortable casting a circle, at least sprinkle a little salted water around your work area, or smudge the area with sage or sandalwood incense.

1. Place the fireproof container in the center of your work space or altar.

2. Dress the candle with the Queen of Pentacles oil and place it in the container.

3. Sprinkle the herbs you've chosen for this spell around the candle in the container.

4. Place the stones on your altar, also arranging them around the container.

5. Light the candle & your incense.

6. Hold the image or the written spell in your hand; close your eyes and still your mind, ground and center. As you're holding this object in your hand, envision it in your mind. Envision it in your mind until it is as real as it would be if you were looking at it. Envision it in your mind until it is as real as it would be if you were experiencing it.

7. Open your eyes and immediately touch the paper to the candle flame. Drop it into the fireproof container with the candle and allow everything to burn down.

8. Once everything has cooled, bury the candle wax and ashes from this spell in the earth upon your property.

Queen of Swords Magick

Magick for the Queen of Swords is often intangible, moving through the mediums of thought and communication. She is connected to the elemental realm of Air, and it's her magick that touches us with a spark of creativity, mental fortitude, and self-expression.

Spells: Communication, Messages, & Ideas
1. Talk to Me

When communication between you and someone within your circle has either petered out for no apparent reason, or stopped abruptly due to disagreements and a falling out, it's important to get that communication flowing as soon as possible to repair the relationship and reaffirm your bond. There's a very easy way to do this.

Take a dab of Queen of Swords oil on the pointer finger of your dominant hand and anoint the bottom of a water glass, moving your finger in a deosil (clockwise) circle, round and round and round she goes.

Fill this glass with a beverage of choice and serve it to the person you are trying to re-establish communication with. The flow of conversation usually begins before the glass is empty.

2. Magickal Messages

If there's someone you wish to get a message to, there's a magickal way to do this. When all other avenues have failed, either because communication is being deliberately blocked, or they are just not listening, write down exactly what it is you have been trying to tell them. Anoint this paper with Queen of Swords oil and tie it outdoors, somewhere where the wind will catch it, preferably in a tree, but a fence-post or a porch rail will work too.

If your message is brief, empower this spell with even more 'oomph' by writing this message on the Queen of Swords tarot card. Punch a hole in one corner of the card and use a yellow thread or narrow ribbon to tie the card to a tree limb.

3. Ignite Your Muse

If you are involved in a creative venture and get stuck for ideas and inspiration, anoint a clear quartz crystal point with Queen of Swords oil, place it in a small pouch with the Queen of Swords card from a tarot deck, and sleep with it beneath your pillow. You will wake the next morning filled with inspiration in the form of dreams, ideas, and images.

Queen of Wands Magick

The Queen of Wands, connected to the elemental realm of Fire, rules magick of fiery unbridled passion with intensity of purpose and a ruthless pursuit of justice. It is her magick that will add swiftness to your spells, giving them focus and accuracy, and the Queen of Wands oil can be added to any spell crafting for this purpose.

Spells for Passion & Justice
1. Light the Fire

And this is exactly what you're going to do, literally. You can do this several ways. You can either do it in a big way and light an outdoor bonfire, or a quaint and cozy fireplace fire, or you can even start a very small flame in your cast iron cauldron or some other small and very fireproof container. (Let me re-emphasize the words "very fireproof".)

At least *three* pieces of the wood or sticks that you add to this fire will be anointed with Queen of Wands oil. When you get your fire going sufficiently, write down on a piece of paper just exactly what aspect of your life needs more passion or energy, or exactly whom it is you wish to ignite with passion. Touch this paper to your lips, and throw it into the flames.

If your message is brief, write it on a Queen of Wands tarot card to add more power and energy to this spell.

2. Sweet Justice

If you are confronted in life with a situation that reeks of unfairness, prejudice, or underhandedness, make a mojo bag aligned with magickal energy to right a wrong, a mojo bag to bring justice.

To this bag add:

1. a stone of apache tear,
anointed with Queen of Wands oil
2. three thorns from a flowering bush
3. a cat's claw, if you have it
4. a small slip of paper on which you've written
the name(s) of those you believe are being nasty, or you can play
it safe and be very general about this. Rather than naming names
refer to 'those who are being unfair', and leave it up to the spirits
to dole out justice in the right place.
5. Queen of Wands tarot card

After all of these ingredients have been added to the mojo bag,
spit in the bag and tie it shut. Keep the bag in a safe and secret
spot.

Queen of Cups Magick

Magick connected to the Queen of Cups will be the most elusive
and ethereal of all. Connected to the elemental realm of Water,
this Queen's energy will rule your dreams and visions, throwing
open the door to magickal realms, infinite possibilities, and
emotions.

Spells for Spirituality & Intuition
1. Spirit Guide Speak

If you wish to connect with your Spirit Guide, if you wish to
receive a message of wisdom, insight, spirituality, and secret
knowledge, you're going to create a mojo bag that you will place
beneath your pillow. Every night, for seven nights in a row, you
will sleep with this bag beneath your pillow. Every morning, you
will jot down in a small notebook any dreams, unusual thoughts,
or visions that came to you on the previous night. On the
morning of the eighth day you will wake, and you will have the
wisdom, inspiration, direction, or answers that you seek.

To create a mojo bag to call your Spirit Guide, add the following items to a small blue or white bag:

1. a stone of moonstone or rose quartz,-anointed with Queen of Cups oil
2. a pinch of mugwort
3. a marigold blossom
4. a talisman for the goddess, such as a Virgin Mary pendent,-or a pendent connected to a pagan deity
5. Queen of cups tarot card

2. Third Eye Sight

To help you open your Third Eye chakra, and thus increase your psychic ability, anoint a blue candle with Queen of Cups oil, roll it in crushed mugwort, set it in a fireproof container, and light it.

As the candle burns, take a dab of Queen of Cups oil on the pointer finger of your dominant hand, and touch it to your third eye.

After the candle has burned itself out, fill a crystal bowl half-full of water, adding the remains of the candle and ashes, and set it outdoors where it will catch the light of a full moon. Place a Queen of Cups tarot card beneath the bowl.

These are only a view examples of the endless array of magick found within the tarot deck. You can use cards for money spells, employment, relationships, and anything else that touches your life and raises your level of awareness. Use the cards on a personal altar for inspiration, meditation, or affirmations; use the cards to connect with the spirits; use the cards to move energy for magickal practices of all kinds.

It would also behoove you to carefully write down your tarot spells in your tarot journal, keeping them safe for future reference.

Amythyst Raine is a professional psychic/clairvoyant. For more information on the services she provides, and to schedule a tarot reading with her, follow this link:

http://ladyamythyst.webs.com

Dodona Books offers a broad spectrum of divination systems to suit all, including Astrology, Tarot, Runes, Ogham, Palmistry, Dream Interpretation, Scrying, Dowsing, I Ching, Numerology, Angels and Faeries, Tasseomancy and Introspection.